They Knew Their God

Volume 5

by
Lillian G. Harvey

UNITED STATES ADDRESS
Harvey Christian Publishers, Inc.
3107 Hwy. 321, Hampton, TN 37658
Tel./Fax (423) 768-2297
E-mail: books@harveycp.com
http://www.harveycp.com

BRITISH ADDRESS
Harvey Christian Publishers UK
11 Chapel Lane, Kingsley Holt
Stoke-on-Trent, ST10 2BG
Tel./Fax (01538) 756391
E-mail: jjcook@mac.com

Original cover design by Vladmir Alkhovik.
Revised for this edition by Melvin Albright, Old Paths Tract Society.

Key to front cover—clockwise beginning at top right: George Herbert, Kate Lee, Miguel Molinos, Samuel Pollard, Jonathan & Rosalind Goforth, Graham Scroggie, Frederick Oberlin, Joseph Alleine, George Matheson.

Printed by
Lightning Source Inc.
La Vergne, TN 37086

Contents

Foreword

WE have added this book to the previous four volumes in the *They Knew Their God* series, hoping by our research to provide the present generation with a knowledge of our tremendous heritage of saints past and present.

Our situation today is much like that which existed in the time of the Judges: "And there arose another generation after them, which knew not the Lord, nor yet the works which he had done for Israel" (Judges 2:10). Such ignorance in those days issued in God's people doing evil and turning to false religions.

Prayer has accompanied our search for little-known giants of faith—people who did exploits because "they knew their God." Such devotion as we read about shames our shallowness and our failure to make a vacuum for God in the busy materialistic scramble for higher living standards. We have expensive homes and luxury cars but know little of the vast riches and resources available to one who takes time to know and understand. Our ideals are so low, and our zeal so lukewarm, and our stocks of grace so pitifully small that we need to remember great saints who all remind us, we too can make our lives sublime, and departing leave behind us, footprints in the sands of time, as Longfellow wrote:

> *Footprints that perhaps another*
> *Sailing o'er life's solemn mane,*
> *Some forlorn and shipwrecked brother*
> *Reading may take heart again.*

My prayer is that you may be lifted to higher ideals and enjoy the exceeding greatness of His power.

Lillian G. Harvey
Yanceyville, North Carolina
April 21, 1998

George Herbert
1593 to 1632

George Herbert

I WILL labor to be like my Master by making humility lovely in the eyes of man," said George Herbert, the Cambridge graduate, to his friends who were chiding him for renouncing all his ambitions in order to give himself to the ministry. In their eyes, their friend was indeed demeaning himself, for they knew that he could boast of much in the way of both natural and acquired accomplishments.

Born in a castle in Montgomery, Wales, Herbert could well be proud of his ancestry, for he belonged to the noble family of the Earl of Pembroke. But he also possessed force of character combined with high mental endowments, which caused him to acquit himself so well at both Westminster and Trinity, Cambridge, that any thoughts of promotion he may have entertained were not without grounds. His position of Public Orator at Cambridge had brought him into contact with royalty. King James I often visited the College and admired the young man; thus court honors were showered upon him. His admirers thought he might well become Secretary of State.

The humble life of Christ, however, had left some impress upon his thinking as shown in a letter written to his mother in her illness when he was twenty-nine:

> If we have riches, we are commanded to give them away; so that the best use of them is, having, not to have them. But perhaps, being above the common people, our credit and estimation calls on us to live in a more splendid fashion. But, Oh God, easily is that answered, when we consider that the blessings in the Holy Scripture

6

are never given to the rich, but to the poor! I never find, "Blessed be the rich," or "Blessed be the noble," but "Blessed be the meek," and "Blessed be the poor," and "Blessed be the mourners, for they shall be comforted."

Only one year later, God in His infinite providence and in a most unusual manner, directed Herbert's life into a totally different channel. The sudden deaths of two of his associates, the Duke of Richmond and the Marquis of Hamilton, followed closely by that of King James, frustrated his chances for future preferment. Thus, at thirty years of age, George Herbert was brought face to face with reality.

Retiring to a quiet country retreat, he seriously considered the life-plan God might have for him. While occupying the position of Public Orator, he had been known to have had a "genteel humor for clothes and court-like company." It was, therefore, not easy for him to lay aside ambitious desires for outward glory in order to become a lowly follower of Christ. So complete, however, was his final decision, that a new birth ushered him into the Kingdom of Heaven, and he was captivated by another King Whose sovereignty never wanes nor ends. To be in the train of His triumph now became the desire of George Herbert. He knew it meant the cross, humiliation, and the way of utter dependence upon One higher than himself.

A stanza of one of his many poems reveals the nature of the spiritual transaction which occurred at this time:

> Oh let Thy sacred will
> All Thy delight in me fulfill!
> Let me not think an action mine own way,
> But as Thy love shall sway,
> Resigning up the rudder to Thy skill.

Although pressured by his mother to become ordained, he would do nothing in haste, so accepted a post as prebender in the parish of Leighton in Huntingdonshire, England. He found the church in a bad state of repair, the roof having fallen in and allowed to remain in that condition for twenty years. The clergy in the neighborhood were licentious and irreverent and, from time to time, used their church for bear-baiting and cock fighting; one minister had even torn down his church, trancforming the chancel into a kennel and the spire intoa dovecote. There was thus ample opportunity for Herbert to display the loveliness of lowliness in face of such irreverence, for humility is reverent. Using personal means with which to restore the church, he left it in beautiful condition when ill health necessitated a change of environment.

The period of sickness which now followed had been caused by his tendency to tuberculosis. He retired to Essex, to the home of his brother, Henry Herbert, a somewhat distinguished figure in the circles in which he moved. Here, he not only refurbished his scanty physical resources, but also found a wife in Jane Danvers who proved to be a true helpmeet during the remaining years of his brief life.

Three months after his marriage, he was ordained vicar in the Church of England. He was sent to the small village of Bemerton, adjacent to the lovely cathedral at Salisbury and also in the proximity of his own family home. He was now thirty-seven years of age and it was at Bemerton that he was to give to the world his lasting treasury of verse and prose.

But writing was by no means his only occupation. In his new parish, he devoted himself assiduously to benefit his parishioners, holding services in the church twice daily. So respected was this humble man, that ploughmen would stop their work to bow in prayer as the bells tolled out the time for service. Friends who would sometimes miss his presence, would find him prostrate on the floor before the altar of his church. The secret of the Lord had been vouchsafed to him when he lost his life that he might find it. Another poem of his will tell us how thoroughly he had learned this lesson of humility:

The bird that soars on highest wing,
    Builds on the ground her lowly nest;
And she that doth most sweetly sing,
    Sings in the shade when all things rest;
In lark and nightingale we see
What honor hath humility.
The saint that wears heaven's brightest crown,
    In deep adoration bends;
The weight of glory bends him down
    The most when high his soul ascends;
Nearest the Throne itself must be
The footstool of humility.

His love and esteem for the Bible can be judged from the following quotation from his own pen:

> The chief and top of the knowledge of the Country Parson consists in the book of books, the storehouse and magazine of life and comfort—the Holy Scriptures. There he sucks and lives. In the Scriptures he finds four things: precepts for life, doctrine for knowledge, examples for illustration, and promises for comfort. But for the understanding of these, the means he useth, are first, a holy life, remembering what his Master saith that, "If any do God's will, he shall know of the doctrine." The second means is prayer; he ever begins the reading of the Scripture with some short inward ejaculation, as, "Lord, open mine eyes that I may see the wondrous things of Thy law" (Psalm 119:18). the third means is a diligent collation of Scripture with Scripture. The fourth means is Commenters and Fathers, which the parson by no means refuseth; he hath one comment at least upon every book of Scripture.[1]

In this connection Barnabas Oley wrote of him:

> Above all things his chief delight was in the Holy Scriptures, one leaf of which he professed he would not part with for the whole world in exchange. That was his wisdom, his comfort, his joy. Out of that he took his motto, "Less than the least of all God's mercies." In that he found that substance, Christ; and in Christ remission of sins; yea, in His Blood he placed the goodness of his good works.[2]

Only two brief years and a few months was George Herbert given to labor in Bemerton before death overtook him when nearing the age of forty. How well he had learned that God designs our weakness to be the conduit for the manifestation of His power. He had also discovered the secret that the wind of the Spirit seeks a vacuum, and that the living waters always find the lowest thresholds.

It is fortunate for posterity that, in his last illness, he turned his thoughts to the manuscript of his complete works and committed it to a friend saying, "Sir, I pray deliver this little book to my dear brother Ferrar and tell him he shall find in it a picture of the many spiritual conflicts that have passed betwixt God and my soul before I could subject mine to the will of Jesus, my Master, in Whose service I have now found perfect freedom. Desire him to read it, and then, if he can think it may turn to the advantage of any dejected poor soul, let it be made public; if not, let him burn it, for I and it are less than the least of God's mercies."[3]

Over three centuries after his death, there has been a revival of interest in George Herbert's poems; they take a prominent place in anthologies of famous English verse. Students in the twentieth century are still studying the poetry of him who, having taken the lowest seat, was told to come up higher. He had lost his life in politics only to find himself occupying an honored place in the host of revered poets and sages of the past.

It is perhaps only fitting that we conclude this sketch of George Herbert by quoting a few stanzas from a poem of his on the humiliation of Christ's incarnation entitled, "The Bag":

> Hast thou not heard, that my Lord Jesus di'd?
> Then let me tell thee a strange story,
> The God of power, as He did ride
> In His majestic robes of glory,
> Resolv'd to light (descend); and so one day
> He did descend, undressing all the way.

The stars His tire of light and rings obtain'd,
The cloud His bow, the fire His spear,
The sky His azure mantle gain'd.
And when they ask'd, what He would wear;
He smil'd, and said as He did go,
He had new clothes a making here below.
When He was come as travelers are wont,
He did repair unto an inn,
Both then, and after, many a brunt
He did endure to cancel sin:
And having giv'n the rest before,
Here He gave up His life to pay our score.

"The only condition for God's mercy is an ability and willingness to receive it."

Miguel Molinos
1627 to 1696

Miguel Molinos

T HE name of Miguel Molinos may not be familiar to many, nor was it to the authors until they came across it in the journals and letters of John Wesley. Then the book, *Golden Thoughts from The Spiritual Guide* by Miguel Molinos came into their hands, which contained a short biographical sketch of this godly priest who dared to teach and practice things contrary to Roman Catholic dogma. His life once more proved the principle that, regardless of nationality or denomination, those who live godly in Christ Jesus cannot escape persecution.

Miguel Molinos was a Spaniard born of a noble family in Minozzi, Aragon, on December 21, 1627. Being duly educated for the priesthood, he took his theological degree and, after a time, went to Rome, anxious to acquire a deeper knowledge of the life of God in man's soul. When forty-eight years of age, he published in Italian his little book, *The Spiritual Guide,* which was later translated into Spanish and found wide circulation. Many who were wearied with outward ceremonies which had proved to be so incapable of giving inner rest, and who were tired of the controversies then raging, found in Molinos' writings the way to "find within the peace denied without."

Molinos taught that the soul of man was the temple of God. It was man's duty to be holy and he could find the fellowship with the God he so much hungered for within the very temple of his being which God had fashioned for Himself. He felt we were the habitation of God, and therefore we should watch against anything which would defile this dwelling-place.

Thou art to know that thy soul is the center, habitation, and kingdom of God. That therefore, to the end the sovereign King may rest on that throne, thou oughtest to take pains to keep thy soul pure, quiet, void and peaceable; pure from guilt and defects; quiet from fears; void of affections, desires and thoughts; and peaceable in temptation and tribulation.

Thou oughtest always then to keep thine heart in peace, that thou mayest keep pure that temple of God, and with a right and pure intention thou art to work, pray, obey, and suffer, without being in the least disturbed, whatever it pleases the Lord to send unto thee.[1]

Possessed of a charming manner and a consistent, holy life, he was a constant contradiction to the prevailing loose standards of his day. Many thought his teaching was almost a new revelation. A group of praying people gathered around him whom he undertook to oversee personally, corresponding with them frequently. It was small wonder that a revival resulted from these efforts.

Eminent men in Rome were attracted to this godly priest, and even Pope Innocent XI would have made him a cardinal, considering him as his spiritual advisor. Bishop Burnet said, "The New Method of Molinos doth so much prevail at Naples that it is believed he hath above 20,000 followers in that city. . . . He hath proposed a great reformation in men's minds and manners. He hath many priests in Italy, but chiefly in Naples."[2]

But such godliness did not escape the notice of the Jesuits, who feared that this would endanger the system. Organized religion has ever been in opposition to a living organism. Again we quote from his biographer:

The disciples of Molinos became noted for their exemplary lives; they were seen to become more devout, to live retired from the frivolity of the world, and to give themselves over to pious works of charity and brotherly sympathy. But they also were seen to be indifferent to those external ways of manifesting piety which the Romanist Church has always insisted on. They seldom went to mass; they set small store by corporeal austerities, relics, image-worship, and pilgrimages. They spent little upon masses for the souls of deceased relations. And above all, they neglected the confessional. . . . Had the movement been allowed to go on, the foundations on which the ecclesiastical system of that church rested might have insensibly crumbled away. The movement was a silent revolution, although it displayed no standard of revolt, and the keen eyes of the Jesuits soon discovered its meaning and to what end it was leading.[3]

If God could be met by any individual in his own room, what need for the confessional or for the priest? The officials of the Church saw that if this thing grew, the money needed to pay her vast retinue of cardinals and to sustain her luxurious courts would not be forthcoming. The Jesuits remembered what the Reformation had done for the German people under Luther; they did not wish anything of that kind to influence Spain and Italy. A popular Jesuit Italian preacher and writer was chosen to attack the principles of Molinos. He wrote a book which, in a clever way, praised Quietism but depreciated its use. This book raised an outcry, for the ruling powers at Rome were strongly in favor of Molinos and his followers. The Inquisition was asked to interfere and as a result the treatise was condemned.

The Jesuits were not to be so easily foiled. They knew that they had a strong influence over Louis XIV of France. This powerful monarch had sins which were dear to him and he was ready to pay any price asked by the Jesuits as a license to continue in them. So Louis' confessor made the king feel that nothing would bring him favor like the condemnation of Molinos and his followers. Cardinal d'Estrées, an intimate of Molinos, was given orders to denounce his former friend and to do it rigorously.

This one-time friend, when thus commanded, did not hesitate to turn traitor; he denounced Molinos to the Inquisition, affirming that his friendship with him had only been in order to detect the heresy which might be found in his friend's beliefs. The Inquisition imprisoned Molinos in 1685; he was now nearing sixty, and as he awaited trial, his followers became panic-stricken.

For almost two years he was kept in close confinement and was made to endure tortures in the hope that confessions might be extracted from him. Some thought the Jesuits had put off the trial, thinking that, after the death of the Pope who was favorable to Molinos, they would be more successful in condemning this man of God.

The letters of the prisoner were used to implicate others whom they sought to intimidate. Friends and followers were promised a fifteen year indulgence if they would attend the trial. The building was crowded, and the face of the condemned man was full of contempt as he stood for three hours listening to the array of evidence against him. The fickle multitude cried, "To the stake! To the stake!" as supposed offenses were read out. Molinos' countenance remained unmoved, nor did he bow his head when the names of Jesus, Mary, and the Holy Sacrament were pronounced.

Few trials have been so unfair as this man's. The charges were not founded on his writings, but on the fact that he was said to have been impure. It is stated that he confessed and abjured. Nobody knows what might have been wrung from the man when enduring tortures such as only the Inquisition was able to inflict. The letters of his enemies, however, who wrote from Rome at that time, "show that he had maintained an unshaken firmness and fortitude. No more cruel or unjust charges could have been brought against any man." From the place of trial, the Church of Minerva, Molinos was led back to his prison in which he stayed until his death on December 28, 1696 when he was seventy years of age.

Molinos' real crime, in the eyes of the Jesuits, was that he and his followers lived pure lives and yet did not go to confessional; they also "set small store by relic-reverence, image worship, and the various superstitious rites which Romanists thought to be essential to religion. The teaching which brought upon him the attack of the Inquisition was . . . that there may be religion without priestcraft, and an approach to God's footstool without first kneeling at a priest's."

These truths which we enjoy today were purchased at a dear price by men of the past, but we do not prize them as we should. Gradually there has arisen within our Protestant Churches a form of Roman Catholicism which frequents the altar and looks to the minister to absolve sin by a pat on the back and a short prayer. This secures eternal life when no life from God has been experienced.

We end with a glorious testimony from this saint of God. May it help to prepare us for the cross which is inevitable if we live pure in heart. It just might be, that before our century ends, we too shall be asked to pay a price for our Christianity in the West.

What great riches is it to be poor! What a mighty honor to be despised! What a height is it to be beaten down! What a comfort is it to be afflicted! What a credit of knowledge is it to be reputed ignorant! And finally, what a happiness of happinesses is it to be crucified with Christ! This is that lot which the Apostle gloried in, "God forbid that I should glory save in the Cross of our Lord Jesus Christ" (Gal 6:14).[4]

The Kingliest Kings

Ho! ye who in the noble work
    Win scorn, as flames draw air,
And in the way where lions lurk
    God's image bravely bear;
Ho! trouble-tried and torture-torn,
The kingliest kings are crowned with thorn.

Life's glory, like the bow in Heaven,
    Still springeth from the cloud:
And soul ne'er soared the starry seven,
    But pain's fire-chariot rode.
They've battled best who've boldest borne;
The kingliest kings are crowned with thorn.

The martyr's fire-crown on the brow
    Doth into glory burn;
And tears that from Love's torn heart flow,
    To pearls of spirit turn.
Our dearest hopes in pangs are born;
The kingliest kings are crowned with thorn.
As beauty in death's cerement shrouds,
    And stars bejewel night,
God's splendors live in dim heart-clouds,
    And suffering worketh night.
The mirkest hour is mother o'morn;
The kingliest kings are crowned with thorn.
                                    —Gerald Massey.

Joseph Alleine

JOSEPH Alleine was one of those two thousand ministers ejected from their pulpits when on August 24, 1662, the Act of Uniformity was put into force. He is best known as author of the book, *An Alarm To The Unconverted*, which, though written over three hundred years ago, is still being printed. A book that can sustain identity over three centuries must have worth in God's sight as well as man's. As Robert Steele states in his short sketch of Alleine:

> His *Alarm to the Unconverted* had an extensive circulation in the seventeenth century, and many were led by it to the strait gate. In the end of last century, a highland minister read a translation of it to his flock, and a great awakening ensued. It is still reprinted and read with profit. His letters and his life have passed through many editions, and his sayings have adorned many a cottage wall, and have been the spiritual bread of thousands.[1]

I had heard that there was a biography of this noble character, and so inquired at Duke University Library. Yes, there was one, I was told, but it was among the rare books not to be taken out of the library. It was possible, however, to microfilm the entire book, which we did. Richard Baxter, who wrote the introduction and compiled the book, thought it best to include the various testimonies of Alleine's relatives and friends, feeling that many voices were better that one in giving a fair and comprehensive portrait of this Puritan saint. The multiplicity, however, and in some instances the repetition of the various accounts, have made it very difficult to write this sketch, and we apologize if, in places, the sketch seems somewhat disjointed.

It is hoped, however, that despite these difficulties, the reader will, like myself, stand utterly amazed at the record of this extremely godly young man who shames us all as to our idea of devotion. I have to admit that he ranks with the very godliest men of the past; in fact, he surpasses the majority. So fervent was Joseph Alleine's devotion to God and so strenuous his life as a minister of the Gospel, that at only thirty-four years of age he exchanged his labors below for his well-earned rest above.

Joseph Alleine was born April 8, 1634 in Devizes, Wiltshire. Again we quote Steele:

> He was descended of a parentage honorable by lineage and by character. His father was a burgess and a counselor, and a man of business in Devizes. He was also a zealous Puritan, and suffered great spoiling of his goods for the sake of his consistent Christian profession. His dying testimony was, "My life is hid with Christ in God."
>
> . . . Soldiers and guns were familiar objects to the youthful Puritan, but his best training was at home, where he had the Christian counsel and pious example of Mr. Tobie Alleine.[2]

When only a boy of eleven, Joseph entered into grace which he maintained until his decease, as one acquainted with Alleine's boyhood writes:

> The first observable zeal of religion that appeared in him, was in the eleventh year of his age, about which time, he was noted to be very diligent in private prayer, and so fixed in that duty, that he would not be disturbed or moved by the coming of any person accidentally into the places of his retirement. . . . While he thus openly began to run his Christian race, his brother, Mr. Edward Alleine, a worthy minister of the Gospel, departed this life: whereupon he earnestly desired to be brought up in preparation to succeed him in the work of the ministry. Which good motion, his father gladly hearkened unto, and speedily prepared to put it in execution. . . .
>
> In the space of about four years, he attained to a very good knowledge in the Latin and Greek tongues, and was by his schoolmaster

adjudged fit for university studies. . . . And when he was about sixteen years old, he was placed in Lincoln College in Oxford. He had not been long in the university, but a Wiltshire place became void in Corpus Christi College. He was chosen scholar of that house. . . .

Never had learning a truer drudge since she kept house in Oxford. . . . At her work he was both day and night thinking all time too little, no pains too much that he spent in her service: when but a schoolboy (as I have heard) he was observed to be so studious, that he was known as much by this paraphrase, "The lad that will not play" as by his name.

Courteous he was and very civil to all acquaintance: but if they came to visit him at studying times, though they were sure enough to find him within, yet withal so busy generally with better company, as to have no leisure to let them in. And if at this they were moved, and murmured, and went away offended with him, he cared not.[3]

Robert Steele gives a few more details of this rather obscure period of Joseph's life:

He went to Oxford in 1649, and entered Lincoln College, over which Dr. Paul Hood presided. Oxford then was Puritan. Cromwell was Chancellor and Dr. John Owen Dean of Christ Church and Vice-Chancellor. The most learned non-conformists were in the highest seats and under them literature, science, philosophy flourished as much as they had ever done within these classic shades.

One of his companions assures us, that it was common for him to work from four o'clock in the morning, and often until one of the next; and that it was as usual for him to give away his commons at least once as it was for others to take theirs twice a day.

He graduated B.A. in June, 1653. He was then only nineteen years of age, but so precocious was his mind and so ripe his scholarship, that he was almost immediately urged to become tutor to his college.[4]

After receiving his degree at nineteen, Joseph accepted a post as tutor to his college where he also acted as chaplain. His advocacy for prayer left a profound impression on his pupils, many of whom later occupied high positions in the Church of England. While walking with them or conversing, he would suggest turning to prayer. He would also visit Oxford jail where infectious diseases were rife.

A close friend of Joseph remembers how he would exhort young students ready to enter university:

> I know, saith he, that you will labor to excel in learning, but be sure to excel in that, so also and especially in holiness, which will render you one of the most useful and amiable creatures in the world. Learning will render you perchance acceptable to men, but piety both to God and men. By that you will shine only on earth to the clods thereof, and perhaps in some obscure corner of it, but this is an orient pearl, which will shine in you on earth and in heaven both to God, angels, and men.[5]

Joseph received various offers of advancement which would have attracted one more ambitious. Some friends even made a special journey to personally persuade the young man to accept their proposition. Oxford University also made him a tempting offer; but he refused them all and, at twenty-one years of age, entered a new phase of his life when he ministered for eight years as assistant to the Rev. George Newton, Presbyterian vicar of St. Mary Magdalene Church in Taunton.

Rev. Newton gives a very touching tribute to his young assistant, which is included in his biography. We prefer to quote from this worthy minister and preserve his seventeenth century style of expression, rather than to spoil it by our own version of his interesting account.

> Mr. Joseph Alleine came to my assistance in the year 1644, being then in the one and twentieth year of his age, and we continued together with much mutual satisfaction till the Black Day.
>
> I soon observed him to be a young man of singular accomplishments, natural and acquired. His intellectuals solid, his memory strong, his affections lively, his learning much beyond the ordinary size, and above all, his holiness eminent, his conversation exemplary; in brief, he had a good head and a better heart.
>
> He spent a considerable part of his time in private converses with God and his own soul; he delighted very much to perform his secret devotions in the view of Heaven and the open air, when he could find advantages fit for his purpose. He used to keep many days alone, and

then a private room would not content him, but (if he could) he would withdraw himself to a solitary house that had no inhabitant in it, and herein he was gratified often by some private friends of his, to whom he did not impart his design: perhaps it was that he might freely use his voice as his affections led him, without such prudential considerations and restraints, as would have been necessary in another place; and that he might converse with God, without any avocation or distraction. . . .

He was ready to instruct and to exhort, and to reprove, which he never failed to do (when he thought it necessary) whatever the event might be: but he performed it usually with such respect, humility, tenderness, self-condemnation, and compassion, that a reproof from him did seldom, if at all, miscarry. . . .

None could live quietly in any visible and open sin, under his inspection; when he came to any house to take up his abode there, he brought salvation with him; when he departed, he left salvation behind him. . . . He was much taken with Monsieur de Renty (whose life he read often) and imitated some of his severities upon better grounds; how often I have heard him to admire (among many other things) especially his self annihilation, striving continually to be nothing, that God may be all. . . .

Men universally almost, do need a spur, but he did rather need a bridle. When other men gave little out of much, he gave much out of little. . . . His heart was an epistle, written not with ink, but with the Spirit of the living God. . . .

He was infinitely and insatiably greedy of the conversion of souls, wherein he had no small success in the time of his ministry; to this end he poured out his very heart in prayer and in preaching; he imparted not the Gospel only but his own soul. His supplications and his exhortations many times were so affectionate, so full of holy zeal, life and vigor, that they quite overcame his hearers. He melted over them, so that he thawed and mollified, and sometimes dissolved the hardest hearts. But while he melted thus, he wasted, and at last consumed himself.

He was not satisfied to spend himself in public, but used constantly to go from house to house, and there, to deal particularly (where he had a free reception) both with the governors and with the children, and with the servants of the household, instructing them especially in the great fundamental necessary truths of the law and of the Gospel, where he observed them to be ignorant, gently reproving them, where he found anything amiss among them. Exhorting them to diligence both in their general and particular callings: entreating them who were defective by any means to set up the worship of God in their houses, and to make them little churches, by constant reading of the Scripture, that so the Word of Christ might deeply dwell among and in them richly, by careful catechizing of the children, and the servants, if the governors were able by frequent meditations, conferences, repetitions of that which they had heard in public; especially by daily prayer, morning and evening, that so they might avoid that dreadful indignation which hangs over, and is ready to be poured out upon the families that call not upon God.

. . . Thus he did wear himself away and give light and heat to others; he usually allowed himself too little sleep to recruit and to repair the spirit which he wasted with waking. His manner was to rise at four o'clock at the utmost, many times before, and that in the cold winter morning that he might be with God betime, and so get room for other studies and employments.

His extraordinary watching, constant cares, excessive labors in the work of his ministry, public and private, were generally apprehended to be the cause of those distempers and decays, and at last, of that ill habit of body whereof in the end he died.

He was the gravest, strictest, most serious, and composed young man, that I had ever yet the happiness to be acquainted with and yet he was not rigid in his principles; his moderation was known to all men that knew him. He held that separation in a church was necessary many times from the known corruptions of it, but allowed not separation from a church where active compliance with some sinful evil, was not made the condition of communion. In this way he frequently declared himself in health and sickness and most expressly in my hearing on his bed of languishing when he was drawing near his Long Home.[6]

Alleine's biographers tell us very little about his personal appearance. One of his most intimate friends, however, does say that "he was of stature tall and erect, of complexion clear and lovely. His countenance being the seat of cheerfulness, gravity and love." This same friend gives a few more interesting insights into Joseph's character:

He was angry and sinned not, by being angry chiefly or only for sin. . . . In summary, what holy Mr. Herbert said of himself, that may be said of him, "That his active soul was as a keen knife in a thin sheath, ever about to cut through and take its flight into the region of souls."[7]

It was far more difficult to him to give than to take a reproof; considering how great wisdom, courage, compassion, self-denial, etc. is required in order to its right discharge.[8]

Therefore did he often delight in his devotions to converse with the fowls of the air, and the beasts of the field, since these were more innocent and less degenerate than man. With streams and plants did he delight to talk, and all these did utter to his attentive ear the praise and knowledge of his Creator.[9]

A godly minister of my past acquaintance used to say, and truly so, that a Gospel which does not open one's purse strings is to be discounted. So it would seem as we study the godly biographies of saints of the past. Alleine was no exception to this as the following letter to his wife, Theodosia, reveals. He was writing regarding the small income he was to receive in his new appointment. The letter also reveals his most exemplary attitude toward his wife; he consulted her in all things, and showed a respect for her opinion even to the point of not engaging in an enterprise if she failed to concur.

My Dear Heart:

By this time I hope thou hast received mine by Martin and also an answer touching their resolution at Taunton. My thoughts have been much upon that business of late, so small as the outward encouragements in point of maintenance are, and methinks I find my heart much inclining that way. I will tell thee the principles upon which I go.

1. I lay this for a foundation, that a man's life consisteth not in the abundance of the things that he possesseth. . . . And certain it is that where men have least of the world, they esteem it least, and live by faith and dependence upon God, casting their care and burden upon Him. . . .

The Holy Ghost seems to make it a privilege to be brought to a necessity of living by faith, as I think, I have formerly hinted to thee, out of Deuteronomy 11:10,11 where Caanan is preferred before Egypt in regard of its dependence upon God for the former and latter rain, which in Egypt they could live without, and have supplies from the river. And certainly could we that are inexperienced, but feel the thorns of those cares and troubles that there are in gathering and keeping much, and the danger when riches increase of setting our hearts upon them, we should prize the happiness of a middle condition much before it. Doubtless, Godliness with contentment, is great gain. Seekest thou great things for thyself? (saith the prophet to Baruch,) Seek them not.

Certainly a good conscience is a continual feast, and enough for a happy life: no man that warreth entangleth himself with the affairs of this life, that he may please Him Who hath chosen him to be a soldier. We should be but little encumbered with the things of this world, and withal free from a world of entanglements, which in a great place committed wholly to our charge, would lie upon our consciences as no small burden.

2. I take this for an undoubted truth, that a dram of grace is better than a talent of wealth, and therefore such a place where our consciences would be free, and we had little to do in the world to take off our hearts and thoughts from the things of eternity, and had the advantages of abundance of means, and the daily opportunities of warming our hearts with the blessed society and conference of heavenly Christians . . . is . . . without comparison, before another place, void of those spiritual helps and advantages. . . .

If we thrive in faith, and love, humility, and heavenly mindedness as above all places I know we are likely to do there, what matter is it though we do not raise ourselves in the world? The thing it may be will be accounted but mean; but alas, let us look upon it with spiritual eye and then we shall pass another judgment of it. Oh, who would leave so much grace, and so much comfort in communion with Christ and His saints, as we may gain there for the possibilities of living with a little more gentility and lordliness in the world?

'Tis a strange thing to see how Christians generally do judge so carnally of things, looking to the things that are seen and temporal, and not the things that will stick by us to eternity. What is it worth a year? Is the maintenance certain and sure? What charges are there like to be? These are the questions we commonly ask first. . . . But alas, though those things are duly to be considered too, yet what good am I like to do! What good am I like to get! (Both which questions I think might be as comfortably answered concerning this as any place in

England.) These should be the main interrogatories, and the chief things we should judge of a place to settle in by.

What if we have but a little in the world? Why then we must keep but a short table, and shall make but a little noise in the world, and must give the meaner entertainments to our friends. Oh, but will not this be abundantly made up if we have a more outward and inward peace, as we may well count we shall have. One dram of saving grace, will weigh down all this. Let others hug themselves in their corn, and wine, and oil, in their fat living, and in their large tables, and their great resort, if we have more of the light of God's countenance, more grace, more comfort, who would change with them?

3. That the best and surest way to have any outward mercy, is to be content to want it. When men's desires are over eager after the world, they must have thus much a year, and a house well furnished, and a wife, and children, thus and thus qualified, or else they will not be content. God doth usually, if not constantly, break their wills by denying them, as one would cross a froward child of his stubborn humor; or else puts a sting into them, that a man had been as good he had been without them, as a man would give a thing to a froppish child, but it may be with a knock on his fingers, and a frown to boot.

The best way to get riches, is out of doubt to set them lowest in one's desires. . . . If we seek the kingdom of God and His righteousness in the first place and leave other things to Him, God will not stand with us for these outwards, though we never ask them we shall have them as over measure. God will throw them in as the vantage. . . .

Certainly, God will never be behindhand with us, let our care be to build His house, and let Him alone to build ours.

4. That none ever was, or ever shall be, a loser by Jesus Christ. Many have lost much for Him, but never did, never shall any lose by Him. Take this for a certainty, whatsoever probabilities of outward comforts we leave, whatsoever outward advantages we balk, that we may glorify Him in our services, and enjoy Him in His ordinances more than other where we could, we shall receive a hundredfold in this life.

'Tis a sad thing to see how little Christ is trusted or believed in the world: Men will trust Him no farther than they can see Him, and will leave no work for faith. Alas, hath He not a thousand ways, both outward and inward, to make up a little outward disadvantage to us? What doth our faith serve for? Have any ventured themselves upon Him in His way, but He made good every word of the promise to them? Let us therefore exercise our faith, and stay ourselves upon the promise, and see if ever we are ashamed of our hope.

5. That what is wanting in the means, God will make up in the blessing. This I take for a certain truth, while a man commits himself and his affairs to God, and is in a way that God put him into: Now if a man have but a little income, if he have a great blessing, that's enough to make it up. Alas, we must not account mercies by the bulk. What if another have a pound to my ounce, if mine be gold for his silver, I will never change with him.

As 'tis not bread that keeps men alive, but the Word of blessing that proceedeth out of the mouth of God, so 'tis not the largeness of the income, but the blessing of the Lord that maketh rich. Oh! if men did but believe this, they would not grasp so much of the world as they do. Well, let others take their course, and we will take ours, to wait upon God by faith and prayer, and rest in His promise. I am confident that that is the way to be provided for; let others toil to enlarge their income (but alas, they will find they go not the right way to work), we will bless God to enlarge our blessing, and I doubt not but we shall prove the gainers.

6. That every condition hath its snares, crosses, and troubles, and therefore we may not expect to be without them wherever we be, only that condition is most eligible that hath fewest and least. I cannot object anything against the proposal of Taunton, but the meanest of the maintenance; but if our income be but short, we can I hope be content to live answerably, we must fare the meanest, that will be all the inconvenience that I know, and truly I hope we are not of the nature of that animal, that hath his heart in his belly.

. . . I have always resolved the place I settled in should be thy choice and to thy content. The least intimation of thy will to the contrary shall overbalance all my thoughts of settling there, for I should account it the greatest unhappiness if I should thus settle and thou shouldest afterwards be discontented by the straitness of our condition. But I need not have wrote this hadst thou not fully signified thy mind already to me, I had never have gone so far as I have.

Well, the Lord Whose we are, and Whom we serve, do with us as it shall seem good unto Him. We are always as mindful as is possible of thee here both together and apart. . . .

I dare not think of settling under sixty pounds at Taunton, and surely it cannot be less. I have written as well as I could on a sudden my mind to thee. I have been so large in delivering my judgment that I must thrust up my affections into a corner. Well, though they have but a corner in my letter, I am sure they have room enough in my heart; but I must conclude. The Lord keep thee, my dear, and cherish thee forever in His bosom. Farewell, my own soul. I am as ever,

Thine own heart, Joseph Alleine.[10]

When we think how Joseph could have had a much larger income as professor at Oxford, and how he turned down this offer, we all the more admire the sacrifices of this godly young man who gave so liberally to others. Although receiving such a small income, the Alleines gave considerable gifts to the poor and to their brethren who were in need, as is told by Richard Alleine, Joseph's father-in-law.

He was eminent in liberality; he not only did but devised liberal things, and by liberal things did he stand; he studied and considered how he might give himself and procure from others, relief for those in want. He gave much alms daily, both in the place where he lived, and wherever he came. When there were collections at any time for pious and charitable uses, he stirred up others to bountiful giving both by word and also by his example.

In the collection for the Fire in London, he gave publicly such a liberal proportion as he thought meet to be an example to others, and (as I came occasionally to understand) lest it should be misjudged had he been known to give more, he gave more than as much again secretly. He distributed much among his relations. His aged father and divers of his brethren with their large families being fallen in decay, he took great care for them all, and gave education to some, pensions to others, portions to others of them. And notwithstanding all this, he had but a very small matter of stock to begin upon, and never above eighty pounds per annum that I know of, and near the one half of his time, not above half so much; only by the industry of his wife who for divers years kept a boarding school, his income was for that time considerably enlarged.

He took great pains in journeyings abroad to many gentlemen and other rich men in the country, to procure a standing supply for such non-conforming ministers as were in want.[11]

His marriage to his cousin, Theodosia, enhanced his already effective ministry. She was known for her fervent piety and many graces. Her father, Richard Alleine, was a pastor in Batcomb.

After living two years with the aged minister, Rev. Newton, they moved to their own home where Theodosia taught fifty to sixty scholars, thirty of whom used to board with the Alleines. This did much to relieve their financial straits and enable them to give liberally to others.

For seven years Joseph labored, not only preaching but calling door-to-door which seemed an innovation to some, as it was not the usual work of the vicar or of his assistant. He would even make a catalog of names in a street and notify each family that he would be visiting the day following. One of the main objectives of this zealous servant of God was to encourage family prayers in each home as Richard Baxter had done in Kidderminster.

But a black day for Britain dawned on August 24, 1662, known as Bartholomew Day in which the Act of Uniformity forced two thousand able ministers from their pulpits. Theodosia writes of this anxious time and of her husband's refusal to sign the Act:

> He seemed so moderate before, that both myself and others thought he would have conformed, he often saying that he would not leave his work for small and dubious matters; but when he saw those clauses of *assent* and *consent*, and *renouncing the covenant*, he was fully satisfied. But seeing his way so plain for quitting the public station he was in, and being thoroughly persuaded of this, that the ejection of the ministers out of their places did not disoblige them from preaching the Gospel, he presently took up a firm resolution to go on with his work in private when his ministry in the church had ceased.[12]

> . . . He presently took up a firm resolution to go on with his work in private, both in preaching and visiting from house to house, till he

should be carried to prison or banishment, which he counted upon the Lord assisting him. . . . It pleased the Lord to indulge him that he went on with his work from Bartholomew Day till May 26th.[13]

This gave seven months for the ejected minister to still preach. In the meantime, Joseph and his faithful wife prepared for the worst:

> We sold up all our goods, preparing for a jail or banishment, where he was desired I should attend him as I was willing to do. It always having been more grievous to think of being absent from him, than to suffer with him.
>
> He would often bless God, and say with holy Mr. Dod that he had a hundred houses for the one that he had parted with; and though he had no goods, he wanted nothing, his Father cared for him in everything, that he lived a far more pleasant life than his enemies, who had turned him out of all. . . . He went from no house that was willing to part with him, nor had he opportunity to answer the requests of half that invited us to their houses.[14]

An arrest warrant finally came and he was sent to prison at Ilchester. He was indefatigable even though imprisoned, giving himself but a few hours of sleep and continuing his early morning rising. Letters to his parishioners poured forth from his prison retreat. He was released after one year and six days on May 20, 1664.

Those who knew Joseph in those days agree that he never recovered from the physical effects of this imprisonment. One of his friends explains:

> He hath often been heard to confess that he knew not what an hour's sickness or indisposition was for thirty years and upward, even until after his first imprisonment to which (as it is elsewhere intimated) it may well be thought that he owed the first and fateful impaires of his healthful vigor. Since which first decay, it may be affirmed that contrarywise for some years together till the period of his life, he scarce knew what was an hour's health.[15]

But a bleaker future faced this saint who, with the joy of the Lord as his constant comfort, had never considered it bleak. In

July 1664, the Five Mile Act, otherwise known as the Conventicle Act, prohibited his travelling far to minister. The sacrificial couple now lived in various houses for two weeks at a time in order to instruct and minister. But one day, when ministers and people had gathered to give him a farewell, justices came and apprehended quite a company of those gathered, as his biographer tells us:

> Mr. Alleine, his wife, his aged father, seven ministers and forty persons were taken away to Ilchester jail. Spiritual exercises sanctified their captivity. But Mr. Alleine's malady was increased by his confinement and when he was liberated at the end of sixty days he was very weak. He retired to his native Devizes to recruit (his strength). On the day after his arrival, his aged father died.[16]

Seizing every opportunity, the imprisoned pastors took turns to minister the Word, and Joseph Alleine preached to those who had come to hear the words of counsel through prison bars.

It was in prison that he wrote books and affectionate letters of encouragement, reproof, and warning, as Robert Steele explains:

> The first of these was his "Call to Archippus," addressed to his suffering fellow-ministers. The next was his admirable exposition of the Assemblies Catechism with an affectionate letter annexed and rules for daily self-examination. He sent a copy of this to every family of his flock in Taunton. He prepared in the mail for them, "A Synopsis of the Covenant." Amidst much discomfort, close confinement and impure air, with an oppressed heart and a feeble frame, Alleine fulfilled his ministry in the prison of Ilchester and made his preaching by the press extend to a greater number than could have assembled in the church of St. Mary Magdalene to hear him.[17]

His wife, Theodosia, tells how he spent himself in the prison for the benefit of others. Did he perhaps realize that his time was short?

> Here as elsewhere, he was a careful redeemer of his time; his constant practice was, early to begin the day with God, rising about four of the clock, and spending a considerable part of the morning in medi-

tation and prayer, and then falling close to his study, in some corner or other of the prison, where he could be private. At times, he would spend near the whole night in these exercises, not putting off his clothes at all, only taking the repose of a hour or two in his nightgown upon the bed, and so up again. . . .

In all his imprisonment, at present, I could not discern his health to be the least impaired, notwithstanding his abundant labors; but cannot but suspect, as the physicians judged, that he had laid the foundation for that weakness, which suddenly after surprised him, and was his death.[18]

Released from prison, Joseph Alleine now faced the serious problems of ill health. His illness started with an extremely tired system which could not digest food. Then he lost the use of legs and arms so that he needed his wife's assistance to write his letters, and to dress and undress. God wonderfully supplied help for Theodosia when, at one period, he needed to be turned forty times in one night. Fourteen women aided her in this nightly task. The kind doctor attended twice daily for twelve weeks, and frequent trips to the Baths helped restore, to some extent, the use of his limbs.

Most people handicapped in this way would have considered themselves excused from further ministerial duties; not so Joseph Alleine, as his biographer explains:

He was able to visit in a chair the almshouses and schools, to distribute books and catechisms, and to give addresses. He also taught a Sabbath school of sixty or seventy poor children at his own lodgings—the first Sunday school in history. His last effort was the transmission of six thousand copies of the Assembly's Catechism to the ministers in Wiltshire and Somersetshire, at the joint expense of himself and a brother minister, as "a thank-offering to God."[19]

His wife gives a few glimpses of her godly husband as he neared the end of his journey:

He constantly gave money or apples to all the children that came to be catechized by him, to engage them, besides all he gave to the teachers, and poor, which indeed was beyond his ability, considering his estate. But I am persuaded he did foresee that his time would be but short; and having made a competent and comfortable provision for me, he resolved to lay up the rest in Heaven; he did often say to me, if he lived ever so long, he would never increase his estate, now I was provided for; he having no children, God's children should have it.[20]

Well, my dear, though we have not our attendants and servants as the great ones and the rich of the world have, we have the blessed angels of God still to wait upon us, to minister to us, and to watch over us while we are sleeping; to be with us when journeying, and still to preserve us from the rage of men and devils.[21]

When I have pleaded with him for more of his time with myself and family, he would answer me: his ministerial work would not permit him to be so constant as he would; for if he had ten bodies and souls, he could employ them all, in and about Taunton; and would say, "Ah my dear, I know thy soul is safe; but how many that are perishing have I to look after? Oh that I could do more for them!"

He was a holy, heavenly, tenderly affectionate husband, and I know nothing I could complain of but that he was so taken up, that I could have but very little converse with him. His love was expressed to me in his great care for me, sick and well; in his provision for me; in his delight in my company, saying often, he could not bear to be from me, but when he was with God, or employed for Him; and that often it was hard for him to deny himself to be so long absent: it was irksome to him to make a meal without me, nor would he manage any affair almost without conversing with me, concealing nothing from me, that was fit for me to know; being far from the temper of those husbands, who hide all their concerns from their wives, which he could not endure to hear of, especially in good men.

He was a faithful reprover of anything he saw amiss in me, which I took as a great evidence of his real good will to my soul; and if in anything he gave me offense, which was but seldom, so far would he deny himself, as to acknowledge it, and desire me to pass it by, professing to me that he could never rest till he had done so; and the like I was ready to do to him, as there was far more reason; by which course, if there was any difference did arise, it was soon over with us.[22]

I perceiving this work, with what he did otherwise to be too hard for him, fearing often he would bring himself to distempers and diseases, as he did soon after, besought him not to go so frequently: "What have I strength for, but to spend for God? What is a candle for but to be burned?". . . . He was exceeding temperate in his diet, though he had a very sharp appetite, yet did he at every meal deny himself, being persuaded that it did much conduce to his health.

". . . Oh wife, I live a voluptuous life, but blessed be God, it is upon spiritual dainties such as the world know not, nor taste not of."[23]

When I have begged him to consider himself and me, he would answer me, he was laying up, and God would repay him; that by liberal things he should stand, when others might fall that censured him; that if he sowed sparingly, he should reap so; if bountifully, he should reap bountifully.[24]

We add a few extracts from his letters, written largely from prison, to show the concern and love he had toward his people:

What progress do you make in sanctification? Doth the house of Saul grow weaker and weaker and the house of David stronger and stronger? . . .

Do you ask for marks how you may know your souls be in a thriving case? . . . If the duties of religion be more easy, sweet and delightful to you. Do you take more delight in the Word than ever? Are you more in love with secret prayer and more abundant in it? Cannot you be content with your ordinary seasons but are ever and anon making extraordinary visits to Heaven? And upon all occasions turning aside to talk with God in some short ejaculations? Are you often darting up your souls heavenwards? Is it meat and drink of you to do the will of God? Do you come off more freely with God and answer His calls and open at His knocks with more alacrity and readiness of mind?

. . . If you grow more vile in your own eyes. Pride is such a choking weed that nothing will prosper near it. Do you grow more out of love with men's esteem and set less by it? . . . Can you rejoice to see others preferred before you?[25]

Welcome prison and poverty, welcome scorn and envy, welcome pain or contempt, if by these God's glory may be most promoted.

What are we for but for God? What doth the creature signify separated from his God? Why just so much as the cipher separated from the figure, or the letter from the syllable, we are nothing or nothing worth, but in reference to God and His ends. . . . I must once again warn you of staying in the suburbs of the city of refuge.

That person that sits down when he hath gotten to that pitch that he thinks will bring him to Heaven, is never like to come thither; grace is one of those things that saith, it never hath enough. Let me urge upon you the Apostle's counsel: "Follow after holiness" (Heb. 12:14).
. . . Righteousness is a breastplate that keeps the vitals, and is sure defense from any mortal wounds (Eph. 6:14).
. . . Did you ever read or hear of a man so mad as to run upon the sword's point, to avoid the scratch of a pin? Or to run upon a roaring cannon, rather than endanger his being wetshod? Why this is the best wisdom of the distracted world, who will sin rather than suffer.

I know whom I have trusted: I am well assured the glass is turned up, and every hour reckoned of our imprisonment, and every scorn and reproach of our enemies is kept in black and white. I believe, therefore do I speak; God is infinitely tender of us, my brethren, though a poor and despicable generation. I value not the pop gun threats of a frowning world; 'tis well with us, we are God's favorites.

Let no man think that to make an outcry upon the wickedness of the times, and to be of the professing party, will serve his turn; many go to Hell in the company of the wise virgins. That no man may be self-deceived let every man be a self-searcher. . . .
There is a three-fold foot that carnal self stands upon: our own wisdom, our own righteousness, our own strength. These three feet must be cut off, and we must learn to have no subsistence in ourselves but only in Christ, and to stand only on His bottom. . . . This holy littleness is a great matter; when we find that all our inventory amounts to nothing but folly, weakness, and beggary; when we set down our selves for ciphers, our gain for loss, our excellencies for very vanities, then we shall learn to live like believers.

I am sure your love to me is, as true friends should be, like the chimneys, warmest in the winter of adversity: And I hope your love to God is much more, and I would that you should abound yet more and more. . . . And let it be seen that you loved Christ and holiness purely for their own sake; that you can love a naked Christ when there is no hope of worldly advantage, or promoting of self interest in following Him.

Take every day some serious turns with death. Think where you shall be a few days and nights hence. Happy he that knew what tomorrow meant for twenty years together. . . .
There is no after-game to be played. What! but one cast for eternity, and will you not be careful to throw that well?

The preacher may seem to be too much like the winter night, very bright, but very cold.

Let him be as the bucket that goes up, though I be as the bucket that goes down.

Brethren, Christ is real in all that He speaks unto you; He is not like a flourishing lover, who fills up his letters with rhetoric, and hath more care of the dress of his speech, than of the truth.

Our advocate is never out of court. Never did cause miscarry in His hand.

Here is no danger of being over-much pleased; neither can the Christian exceed his bounds in over-valuing his own riches, and happiness in Christ.

There are three things which I beseech you carefully to beware of. First, Lest while Christ is in your mouths, the world run away with your hearts. . . .
Remember, I beseech you, that the oxen, the farm, wife, merchandise, all of them lawful comforts, did as effectually keep men from a sound and saving closing with Christ, as the vilest lusts of the worst of men. Whatever you find your hearts very much pleased in, and in love with, among these earthly comforts, set a mark upon that thing, and remember that there lies your greatest danger. What you love most, you must fear most, and think often with yourselves, "This if anything is like to be my ruin." Oh, the multitudes of professors that perish

forever by the secret hand of this mortal enemy, I mean the over-valuing of earthly things.

Beloved, I despair of ever bringing you to salvation without sanc-tification. . . . Labor to get a saving change within, or else all exter-nal performances will be to no purpose.

Every grain shall produce a crown; and every tear shall bring forth a pearl; and every minute in pain or prayers, an age of joy and glory.

He is not a Christian indeed that cannot be content to tarry for his preferment in another world.

Nothing is done for God, but thou shalt hear of it again. What-ever is not done for God, is but so much lost.

I am never quiet until I am in my old way of communion with God.

Oh, be as solicitous every day to keep your praying times which are a thousand times more necessary than a time to eat in or sleep.

See to it that you do not rest in a worldly religion; to give God your knee, while the world carries away your heart.

Do I think Heaven will drop into my mouth? That glory and immortality will be gotten with a wet finger, with cold prayers, and heartless wishes, while the world carries the main of my heart? Do I think to be crowned, and yet never fight? To get the race, and never run? To enter the strait gate, and never strive? To overcome princi-palities and powers, and never wrestle?

God abhors that the proud should come near Him; oh labor, what-ever you do, for a humble heart; be little, be vile in your own eyes; seek not after great things; be poor in spirit. Without this, Heaven will be no place for you. God will be no friend to you.

I find no enemy so dangerous as self.

> For my part I thought that God took us upon His knee to whip us, but He took us upon His knee to dandle us.[26]

Perhaps one of Alleine's most moving letters is written to his cousin only one month before his death. In it, he shows a deep concern for her and her husband because of their worldly outlook; he wishes to ensure that their sense of earthly security is balanced by a deep awareness of unseen and eternal truths, and an assurance that they were indeed citizens of the heavenly Kingdom. It is dated Oct. 21, 1668.

Dear Cousin:

> Though I have been in the valley of the shadow of death, though I have had more than one foot in the grave, and have been in deaths often, yet the love and remembrance of you ever liveth on my heart. I have long had neither feet to walk nor hands to write, yet I have borrowed hands as you see, rather than I would stay any longer from warning and admonishing of you.
>
> Dear cousin, that soul of yours, that precious immortal soul is of no light value with me! I pray hard for its salvation. I have a godly fear for you, lest your soul should miscarry in a crowd of worldly business and of earthly cares. Ah, my dear niece, it comforts me that you are so settled for this world, and are in want of nothing, I bless the Lord for this, but methinks this doth not satisfy me. Oh, that I could be sure that you were once safe settled in Christ; though you are, I trust, comfortably furnished with earthly things, yet in this you are but half provided for. Have you a treasure in Heaven? Have you laid hold on eternal life? Have you made sure work for everlasting? Have you passed the straits of the new birth? Do you bear upon you the marks of the Lord Jesus?
>
> If you shall pass by a sumptuous fabric, and a great lordship, and should lay claim to all as your inheritance, and please yourself with the hopes of enjoying all this when you had nothing to show, no writing, no evidence to produce, as a grounds for any such hope, would not everyone say, this were a piece of strange vanity and imprudence. Much greater folly is it to promise ourselves a part in para-

dise, and rest satisfied in a mere persuasion that we are the heirs of Heaven, when we cannot prove our title from the Book of God, nor produce from within ourselves, the sure and certain marks of the children of God.

Ah, dear cousin, rouse up yourself, make conscience to deal plainly and freely with your soul. Say within yourself, I have hopes for Heaven. But where are my grounds and evidences? Do I not build without a foundation? Do I venture my salvation upon mere uncertainties? What have I, what do I more than others? I pray, I hear, I read. But may not a mere hypocrite do all this? I run not with others into the wretched practice of lying, and cozening, whoredom, and the like. But what is this more than a Pharisee may have to say for himself? Can I prove by Scripture my claim for Heaven? Can I produce chapter and verse to justify myself?

Oh, cousin, fear lest the promise being left of entering into rest, you should by any mistakes, or self-deceits fall short through unbelief. Fear lest you should take counters of gold, or some common workings for saving grace. Oh, there is a world of counterfeit going. Multitudes perish by mistakes, and wait in hell, whilst they dreamt they were in Heaven.

The tempter is very subtle and will sure deceive if he can. Your heart is deceitful above all things, and is willing to cheat you if it can. Therefore am I engaged so earnestly to call upon you, as one that watcheth for your soul, to arise speedily and to set roundly to your work. Oh, consider your danger, and work out your salvation with fear and trembling. Away with these lazy prayers. Away with these cold and heartless professions. Away with this drowsy, lifeless, listless religion. Bestir yourself to purpose for your soul before it be too late. Search your conscience as with candles. Be jealous of yourself. Consider now is your time. What you do, you must do quickly. The patience of God is waiting; Christ is knocking; the Spirit of God is striving, and death is at the door.

Oh now take your opportunity and take heed lest a slothful heart, and the cares of this world, or a presumptuous confidence that all is well and safe already, should at last shut you out of the Kingdom of God.

I cannot write distinctly to your husband, but I beseech you to call upon him to set his heart to these counsels which I have written to you. I earnestly entreat him to make religion his business, and to look heedfully to it that the gain of the world prove not the loss of his soul. I desire him that closet and family prayers, and weekly catechizing of his household, and strict sanctifying of the Sabbath, and reading of the Scriptures, singing of Psalms, repeating of sermons, and diligent attendance upon powerful preaching may be his continual exercises. So his house may be a little church, and God may be like to dwell in his family. Pray give me to understand what is done of these things, for I have a zeal for your welfare, and that you and your household should serve the Lord, that you may enter into His rest, and carry children, and servants, and friends, and all to Heaven with you.

As to my own estate, I have lost all my limbs, and about this twelvemonths useless and been again and again under the sentence of death, but was brought in a horse lift to Bath where God hath wonderfully restored me, so that I can feed myself and go alone and speak with a little more freedom. Oh, love the Lord, praise the Lord for me; notwithstanding I continue weak and have not strength to write, yet I could not tell how to die in silence from you, but have made use of a friendly hand to send these counsels and calls after you, which I beseech you to accept in the fear of God, for it is not unlike that they may be my last to you that ever you may receive. I now commend you to the Lord, and with mine own and my dear wife's love to you both, rest,

Your loving and careful uncle,

Joseph Alleine.[27]

For some time before his death, Mr. Alleine's mind was in Heaven, as Theodosia tells us: "But what time I had with him he always spent in heavenly and profitable discourse, speaking much of the place he was going to, and his desires to be gone: one morning as I was dressing him, he looked up to heaven and smiled, and I, urging him to know why, he answered me thus, "Ah, my love, I was thinking of my marriage day. It will be shortly. Oh what a joyful day will that be! Will it not, thinkest thou, my dear heart?"

Theodosia was a faithful nurse right till the end. She witnessed a torturing convulsion in November which lasted for hours. Doctor and bystanders thought he would take his flight, but he came out of it to speak for sixteen hours. About three in the afternoon of the day in which he went to be with his beloved Master, he was seen to have some conflict with Satan, for he uttered these words: "Away thou foul fiend, thou enemy of all mankind, thou subtle sophister, art thou come now to molest me! Now, I am just going! Now I am so weak, and death upon me. Trouble me not, for I am none of thine! I am the Lord's, Christ is mine, and I am His: His by covenant; I have sworn myself to be the Lord's, and His I will be: therefore be gone."

Then, on November 17, 1668, Joseph Alleine passed out of great tribulation into the rest for warriors. Not one thing had he withheld from God or from the oversight of his flock. A truly caring shepherd, he had heard his "Well done, good and faithful servant, enter thou into the joy of thy Lord." The epitaph on his tombstone very aptly sums up his whole life: "Here lies God's and Taunton's sacrifice."

We close with a poem from Richard Baxter which reveals the hardships suffered by the ministers who were excluded from their pulpits in 1662:

> Must I be driven from my books?
>   From house and goods and dearest friends?
> One of Thy sweet and precious looks,
>   For more than this will make amends!
>
> As for my house, it was my tent,
>   While there I waited on Thy flock;
> That work is done, that time is spent,
>   There neither was my home nor stock.

Would I in all my journey have,
　　Still the same inn and furniture?
Or ease and pleasant dwellings crave,
　　Forgetting what Thy saints endure?

My Lord hath taught me how to want
　　A place wherein to put my head;
While He is mine, I'll be content
　　To beg or lack my daily bread.

Heaven is my roof, earth is my floor,
　　Thy love can keep me dry and warm,
Christ and Thy bounty are my store;
　　The angels guard me from all harm.

As for my friends, they are not lost;
　　The several vessels of Thy fleet,
Though parted now, by tempests tost,
　　Shall safely in the haven meet.
　　　　　　　　—Richard Baxter.

Birthplace of
John Fletcher

John Fletcher
1729-1785

Plaque outside
Madeley Vicarage

John Fletcher

OVERLOOKING Lake Leman near Nyon, Switzerland, stood the noble and spacious villa surrounded by walled gardens and vineyards which housed the highly respected Fletcher family. Into this noble household, boasting itself of being a branch of the Earls of Savoy, was born the youngest child on September 12, 1729, John William Fletcher. This child was destined under God to become one of the saintliest and humblest of men ever to grace the Christian Church.

The Fletchers gave their sons a thorough education, and John was sent along with a brother to Geneva where he pursued his studies with an assiduity that was striking in one so young. All day he would study industriously, and at night he borrowed hours from sleep to write out what he had observed and learned throughout the day. This gave him a classical style of writing which later characterized his literary works.

His consciousness of God began at an early date:

> From the time I first began to feel the love of God shed abroad in my soul, which was, I think, at seven years of age, I resolved to give myself up to Him, and to the service of His Church, if ever I should be fit for it; but the corruption which is in the world, and that which was in my heart, soon weakened if not erased those first characters which grace had written upon it.
>
> However, I went through my studies with a design of entering the ministry; but afterwards, upon serious reflection, feeling I was unequal to so great a burden, and disgusted by the necessity I should be under to subscribe to the doctrine of predestination, I yielded to the desire of those of my friends who would have me go into the army. But just

before I was quite engaged in a military employment, I met with such disappointments as occasioned my coming to England.[1]

When God separates a man or woman for some special work, it would seem that the forces of both good and evil are very evidently at work in that person's life. Like many others who were to become greatly used by God, John Fletcher passed through hairbreadth escapes. Being a lover of climbing, swimming, and rowing on the lake, he experienced numerous remarkable deliverances from the jaws of death and it seemed that Satan was vainly attempting to frustrate the divine plan.

On the other hand, there were many providences which protected John and kept him from pursuing any path other than the one designed by his heavenly Father. For example, when he was determined to join the army even against his parents' wishes, God interfered with his plans in a remarkable manner. Unable to persuade his parents to relent in their desire for him to enter the ministry, John went to Lisbon without their consent, where he gathered a group of like-minded young Swiss around him. Together they agreed to serve the King of Portugal on a Man-of-War bound for South America. The day the ship was to sail, the maid serving his breakfast accidentally dropped a tea kettle of boiling water on his leg, scalding him so badly that he was confined to bed. The Man-of-War left without him and incidentally never was heard of again.

An uncle who was an officer in the Dutch army secured a commission for him, and the youth set out for Flanders. Upon his arrival, hostilities had ceased, and the death of his uncle within a few weeks closed the door to anything further in the Army. So the young Swiss made his way to England and immediately sought out someone who could teach him English. A Mr. Burchell, who had a Boarding School in Middlesex and who later moved to Hatfield, was recommended to him. John stayed eighteen months with Mr. Burchell where he diligently studied English and all the branches of classical literature.

He next moved to Shropshire, where a post had been procured for him by a French minister as tutor to the two sons of Mr. Hill who lived at Tern Hall. More than mere man had a hand in securing twenty-three year old John this appointment, for within ten miles of Tern Hall lay Madeley, where he was to spend the remainder of his life. It was also through this post as tutor that he first met the Methodists whose ministry brought light to the young tutor who had "none to take him by the hand and lead him forward in the ways of God."

His employer, being a Member of Parliament, had to take frequent trips to London and took his family with him. On one of these journeys, they stopped at St. Albans to exchange horses. Fletcher went for a walk and lingered so long that Mr. Hill traveled on without him but left a horse for John to follow afterwards. When later asked by the family the reason for his delay, John replied: "I met with a poor old woman who talked so sweetly of Jesus Christ that I knew not how the time passed away."

This made Mrs. Hill remark, "I shall wonder if our tutor does not turn Methodist by and by."

"Methodist, Madam," John inquired, "Pray what is that?"

"The Methodists," she replied, "are a people who do nothing but pray; they are praying all day and all night."

"Then, by the help of God, I will find them out, if they be above ground," was the young man's response. Find them he did, and before long was admitted into the Society. When in London, he attended the class meeting held by Mr. Edwards, for whom he retained a respect to the end of his life.

John Fletcher's mode of religious life at this time is best recounted by his biographer:

> He counted much upon the dignity of human nature and was ambitious to act in a manner becoming his exalted ideas of that dignity. And here he outstripped the multitude in an uncommon degree. He was rigidly just in his dealings, and inflexibly true to his word; his sentiments were liberal and his charity profuse; he was prudent in his

conduct and courteous in his deportment; he was frequent in sacred meditations, and was a regular attendant at public worship.[2]

How devastating to human pride was the conviction that now seized this moral young man of the utter depravity of his heart, and his complete inability, by works of his own, to be reconciled to God. He could not, even by means of the utmost rigorous austerities, subdue his evil nature. The more he tried the worse he felt.

Writing of this experience to his brother he said: "This will appear incredible, except to those who have discovered that the heart of unregenerate man is nothing more than a chaos of obscurity, and a mass of contradictions."[3]

At twenty-five years of age this searcher after God recorded in his diary:

Instead of going straight to Christ, I have wasted my time in fighting against sin with the dim light of my reason and the mere use of the means of grace—as if the means would do me good without the blessing and power of God. I fear my knowledge of Christ is only speculative and does not reach my heart. I never had faith, and without faith it is impossible to please God. Therefore, all my thoughts, words, and works, however specious before men, are utterly sinful before God. And if I am not washed and renewed before I go hence, I am lost to all eternity. . . .

I would here observe that anger in particular seemed to be one of the sins I could not overcome. So I went on sinning and repenting, and sinning again; but still calling on God's mercy through Christ.

I was now beat out of all my strongholds. I felt my helplessness, and lay at the feet of Christ. I cried, though coldly, yet I believe sincerely, "Save me, Lord, as a brand snatched out of the fire. Give me justifying faith in Thy blood. Cleanse me from my sins, for the devil will surely reign over me until Thou shalt take me into Thy hand." I seldom went to private prayer, but this thought came into my mind, "This may be the happy hour when thou wilt prevail with God." But still I was disappointed. . . .

I heard an excellent sermon on these words, "being justified by faith, we have peace with God through our Lord Jesus Christ." I heard it attentively, but my heart was not moved in the least. . . . I found relief in Mr. Wesley's journal, where I learned that we should not build on what we feel, but go to Christ with all our sins and our hardness of heart.[4]

Intending to partake of the sacrament, John studied a hymn and prayed it over many times. He then retired for the night but was awakened by a terrible dream in which he had committed grievous sins. He awoke amazed. Rising, he knelt to pray with more faith than was usual. When tempted with his usual besetting sin, he felt that there was not even a ruffle in his spirit. When later two or three temptations came to him, he observed that there was peace in his soul; he attributed the change to the Lord's working in his heart.

In the evening, while reading of the experiences of other Christians, he found there was a similarity between his case and theirs and re-emphasized the sermon he had heard on justifying faith. Wondering, however, if he might not be deluded, he remained on his knees until one o'clock in the morning, when he opened his Bible at Psalm 55:22, "Cast thy burden on the Lord and he shall sustain thee; he will not suffer the righteous to be moved." Opening his Bible again, he was comforted with Deuteronomy 31: "I will be with thee, I will not fail thee, neither forsake thee; fear not, neither be dismayed."

His diary reads: "With this comfortable promise I shut up my Bible, being now perfectly satisfied. As I shut it I cast my eye on that word, 'Whatsoever ye shall ask in my name, I will do it.' So having asked grace of God to serve Him till death, I went cheerfully to take my rest."[5]

The words of a hymn were applied with power to his heart; they were these:

> Seized by the rage of sinful men,
> I see Christ bound, and bruised, and slain;
>   'Tis done, the martyr dies!
> His life to ransom ours is given,
> And lo! the fiercest fire of heaven
>   Consumes the sacrifice.
>
> He suffers both from men and God,
> He bears the universal load
>   Of guilt and misery!

He suffers to reverse our doom,
And lo, my Lord is here become,
The Bread of Life to me!

The newly born convert now followed after God with the same intensity with which he had pursued his studies. Two whole nights each week he sat up for meditation, prayer, and study. Having been once threatened with consumption, he had been advised by his doctor to adopt a vegetable diet. Now wishing to live more simply, he took this advice and lived on vegetables, bread, milk, and water. This frugal diet enabled him to avoid sitting at the table and dining with the Hills and their company. In later life, however, Mr. Fletcher observed to his wife that if he had his life to live over again he would treat his body more kindly in regard to sleep and meat. For he reasoned, "I have sometimes observed that when the body is brought low, Satan gains an advantage over the soul. It is certainly our duty to take all the care we can of our health. But, at that time, I did not seem to feel the want of sleep I deprived myself of."[6]

Mr. Hill sought to find a vicarage in which Mr. Fletcher might serve His Master. The following conversation taken from his biographer, Jabez Marrat, is worth recording:

> Mr. Hill informed him he could have the living of Dunham in Cheshire, adding, "The parish is small, the duty light, the income good (£400 per annum) and it is situated in a fine, healthy, sporting country."
>
> The reply was: "Alas! Sir, Dunham will not suit me; there is too much money and too little labor."
>
> "You clergymen," said Mr. Hill, "make such objections; it is a pity to decline such a living, as I do not know that I can find you another. What shall we do? Would you like Madeley?"
>
> "That, Sir," said Fletcher, "would be the very place for me."
>
> "My object," replied Mr. Hill, "is to make you comfortable in your own way. If you prefer Madeley, I shall find no difficulty in persuading the present Vicar to exchange it for Dunham, which is worth more than twice as much."[7]

In a letter to Charles Wesley, whose advice he had sought about taking Madeley as his parish, he opened his heart concerning the struggles he was experiencing regarding his future. Charles had advised him "not to resist providence but to follow its leadings" but, as Mr. Fletcher explains, that, too, had its difficulties:

> I am, however, inwardly in suspense. My heart revolts at the idea of being here alone, opposed by my superiors, hated by my neighbors, and despised by all the world. Without piety, without talent, without resolution, how shall I repel the assault and surmount the obstacles which I foresee, if I discharge my duty at Madeley with fidelity? On the other hand, to reject this presentation, to burn the certificate, and to leave in the desert the sheep whom the Lord has evidently brought me into the world to feed, appears to me nothing but obstinacy and refined self-love. I will hold a middle course between these extremes; I will be wholly passive in the steps I must take, and active in praying the Lord to deliver me from the Evil One, and to conduct me in the way He would have me to go.
>
> If you see anything better, inform me of it speedily; and, at the same time, remember me in all your prayers, that if this matter be not of the Lord, the enmity of the Bishop of Lichfield, who must counter-sign my testimonials; the threats of the Chaplain of the Bishop of Hereford, who was a witness to my preaching at West Street; the objections drawn from my not being naturalized, or some other obstacle, may prevent the kind intentions of Mr. Hill. Adieu.[8]

In 1760, when Fletcher was but thirty-one years of age, he moved to Madeley where God was to bless his ministry abundantly for the next twenty-five years, and extend that ministry beyond his death through his faithful and holy wife, Mary Fletcher, for another twenty-five years. Surely few mining villages were to be shepherded by such faithful souls as was this blaspheming, licentious, bull-baiting and ignorant population. They had little respect for man, and less reverence for piety. Certainly Mr. Fletcher's charge would not be an easy one. His biographer describes the village in its moral and spiritual aspects and Mr. Fletcher's reaction to such conditions:

> Celebrated for the extensive works carried on within its limits, Madeley was remarkable for little else than the ignorance and profaneness of its inhabitants, among whom respect to man was as rarely to be

observed as piety toward God. In this benighted place the Sabbath was openly profaned, and the most holy things contemptuously trampled under foot; even the restraints of decency were violently broken through, and the external form of religion held up as a subject of ridicule. . . .

It was a common thing in his parish for young persons of both sexes to meet at stated times for the purpose of what is called recreation, and this recreation usually continued from evening to morning, consisting chiefly in dancing, reveling, drunkenness, and obscenity. These licentious assemblies he considered as a disgrace to the Christian name, and determined to exert his ministerial authority for their total suppression.

He has frequently burst in upon these disorderly companies with a holy indignation, making war upon Satan in places peculiarly appropriated to his service. Nor was his labor altogether in vain among the children of dissipation and folly. After standing the first shock of their rudeness and brutality, his exhortations have been generally received with silent submission, and have sometimes produced a partial, if not an entire reformation in many who were accustomed to frequent these assemblies.[9]

In a letter to Charles Wesley dated March 10, 1761, he writes:

A few days ago, I was violently tempted to quit Madeley: the spirit of Jonah had so seized upon my heart that I had the insolence to murmur against the Lord. But the storm is now happily calmed, at least for a season. Alas! what stubbornness is there in the will of man; and with what strength does it combat the will of God under the mask of piety when it can no longer do so with the uncovered, shameless face of vice.

. . . I know not what to say to you of the state of my soul: I daily struggle in the slough of despond, and I endeavor every day to climb the hill difficulty. I need wisdom, mildness, and courage; and no man has less of them than I. Oh Jesus, my Savior, draw me strongly to Him Who giveth wisdom to all who ask it, and upbraideth them not! As to the state of my parish, the prospect is yet discouraging. New scandals succeed those that wear away, but offenses must come: happy shall I be, if the offense cometh not by me![10]

In another letter he writes:

When I first came to Madeley, I was greatly mortified and discouraged by the smallness of my congregations; and I thought that if some of our friends at London had seen my little company, they would have triumphed in their own wisdom. But now, thank God, things are altered in that respect, and last Sunday I had the pleasure of seeing some in the church yard who could not get into the church.[11]

Later he writes on October 12:

My church begins not to be so well filled as it has been, and I account for it by the following reasons: the curiosity of some of my hearers is satisfied, and others are offended by the Word; the roads are worse, and if it shall ever please the Lord to pour His Spirit upon us, the time is not yet come; for instead of saying, "Let us go up together to the house of the Lord," they exclaim, "Why should we go and hear a Methodist?" I should lose all patience with my flock if I had not more reason to be satisfied with them than with myself. My own barrenness furnishes me with excuses for theirs; and I wait the time when God shall give seed to the sower and increase to the seed sown. In waiting that time, I learn the meaning of this prayer, "Thy will be done."[12]

There seemed to be no man so loving in his disposition to both God and man as was John Fletcher as his biographer tells us:

At one season he would open his mouth in blessings; and at another he would appear like his Lord amid the buyers and sellers with the lash of righteous severity in his hand. But, in whatever way he exercised his ministry, it was evident that his labors were influenced by love, and tended immediately either to the extirpation of sin or the increase of holiness. . . . Like a vigilant pastor, he daily acquainted himself with the wants and dispositions of his people, anxiously watching over their several households and diligently teaching them from family to family . . . esteeming no man too mean, too ignorant, or too profane to merit his affectionate attention. He condescended to the lowest and most unworthy of his flock, cheerfully becoming the servant of all, that he might gain the more."[13]

He possessed such intensity of love that he would go about the village early Sunday morning with a bell to waken the inhabitants and remind them of their need to attend the place of worship. We see him taking down the pewter from his shelves to assist the poor in their dire need. We see him giving himself day by day to go house to house, inquiring about the soul's welfare. We watch him at the sick or dying bed of his parishioners at any time of day or night, spending and being spent for others. We follow him through his faithful preaching, giving his audience the Word of Life.

Love cannot be so intense in its nature, however, without manifesting an equally intense hatred for evil; for the one, by its very nature, produces the other. Mr. Fletcher had seen the awful ravages of sin and knew the immensity of the love that brought Christ down from above to make an atonement for that sin, and by His death procure a remedy for the curse of sin brought about by the fall. To only present the loving side of this man of God without showing his hatred for the sin of rejecting Christ's cure, would be to only show but one side. Man of himself cannot produce the tremendous blend of mercy and truth, love and hate. Only the blessed Holy Ghost can mix together such seemingly unlike emotions, and if we do not also see John Fletcher as one who uttered fearful warnings and utterances under the influence of the Spirit of God, we only see one side of the man. The following episode will suffice to illustrate:

> This evening I have buried one of the warmest opposers of my ministry, a stout, strong young man, aged twenty-four years. About three months ago he came to the church yard with a corpse but refused to come into the church. When the burial was over, I went to him and mildly expostulated with him. His constant answer was that he had bound himself never to come to church while I was there; adding that he would take the consequences, etc. Seeing I got nothing, I left him, saying with uncommon warmth (though as far as I can remember without the least touch of resentment), "I am clear of your blood; henceforth it is upon your own head. You will not come to church upon your legs, prepare to come upon your neighbors' shoulders." He wasted from that time, and to my great surprise hath been buried on the spot where we were when the conversation passed between us. When I visited him in his sickness, he seemed tame as a wolf in a trap. Oh may God have turned him into a sheep in his last hours![14]

Two important events occurred during these twenty-five years in Madeley apart from and previous to his marriage. In 1768, when

Fletcher was nearing forty years of age, he returned from a visit to his native land where he had opportunities of service for God. Trevecca College was opened by the Countess of Huntingdon about this time for young men wishing to devote themselves to Christian work. They could remain at the college for three years. Knowing the piety of Mr. Fletcher, Lady Huntingdon invited him to be superintendent of the college, and granted him the right to be present only at intervals so that he might not fail in his duties at Madeley. He did this work without remuneration in order to help train young men for ministry. The students and all the staff revered their overseer. A few words from Mr. Benson describing Mr. Fletcher's labors will give our reader a minute description:

> Here it was that I saw, shall I say, an angel in human flesh? I should not far exceed the truth if I said so. But here I saw a descendant of fallen Adam so fully raised above the ruins of the fall, that though by the body he was tied down to earth, yet was his whole conversation in heaven, yet was his life, from day to day, hid with Christ in God. . . . And as to others, his one employment was to call, entreat, and urge them to ascend with him to the glorious source of being and blessedness. He had leisure comparatively for nothing else. Languages, arts, sciences, grammar, rhetoric, logic, even divinity itself as it is called, were all laid aside when he appeared in the school room among the students. His full heart would not suffer him to be silent. He must speak, and they were readier to hearken to this servant and minister of Jesus Christ than to attend to Sallust, Virgil, Cicero, or any Latin or Greek historian or philosopher they had been engaged in reading. And they seldom hearkened long before they were all in tears, and every heart catched fire from the flame that burned in his soul.
>
> These seasons generally terminated in this: being convinced that to be filled with the Holy Ghost was a better qualification for the ministry of the Gospel than any classical learning (although that too be useful in its place), after speaking a while in the school room, he used frequently to say, "As many of you as are athirst for this fullness of the Spirit, follow me into my room." On this, many of us have instantly followed him, and there continued for two or three hours, wrestling like Jacob for the blessing, praying one after another till we could bear to kneel no longer. This was not done once or twice, but many times."[15]

A letter of Mr. Fletcher's dated January, 1771, explains why his ministry there was of such brief duration:

> For my part, I am no party man. In the Lord I am your servant, and that of your every student. But I cannot give up the honor of being connected with my old friends, who, notwithstanding their failings, are entitled to my respect, gratitude, and assistance, could I occasionally give them any. Mr. Wesley shall always be welcome to my pulpit, and I shall gladly bear my testimony in his, as well as in Mr. Whitefield's. But if your Ladyship forbid your students to preach for the one, and offer them to preach for the other at every turn, and if a Master is discarded for believing that Christ died for all; then prejudice reigns; charity is cruelly wounded; and party spirit shouts, prevails, and triumphs.[16]

"Rather suffer in silence," wrote Fletcher to another, "than make a noise to make the Philistines to triumph. Take care, my dear sir, not to make matters worse than they are, and cast the mantle of forgiving love over the circumstances that might injure the cause of God, so far as it is put into the hands of that eminent lady, who hath so well deserved of the Church of Christ."[17]

In a further letter he states his convictions about leaving Trevecca:

> As I entered it a free place, I must quit it the moment it is a harbor for party spirit.
> As I am resolved to clear up this matter, or quit my province, I beg you will help me to as many facts and words, truly done, and really spoken, as you can; whereby I may show (to the parties concerned at Trevecca) that false reports, groundless suspicions, party spirit against Mr. Wesley, arbitrary proceedings, and unscriptural impulses hold the reins and manage affairs in the college; as also the balance of opinions is not maintained, and Mr. Wesley's opinions are dreaded and struck at more than deadness of heart and a wrong conduct.[18]

Again Fletcher cautions:

> Do not make matters worse than they are; I fear they are bad enough. So far as we can, let us keep this matter to ourselves. When you speak of it to others, rather endeavor to palliate than aggravate

what hath been wrong in your opposers. Remember that great lady has been an instrument of great good, and that there are great inconsistencies attending the greatest and best of men. Possess your soul in patience; see the salvation of God; and believe, though against hope, that light will spring out of darkness. I am with concern for you and that poor college, yours in Jesus, J. F.[19]

Soon after writing the above, Fletcher returned to the college on a visit and wrote to a friend:

On my arrival at the college, I found all very quiet, I fear through the enemy's keeping his goods in peace. While I preached the next day, I found myself as much shackled as ever I was in my life. And after private prayer, I concluded I was not in my place. . . . The same day I resigned my office to my Lady and on Wednesday to the students and the Lord. . . . Last Friday I left them all in peace, *the servant,* but no more the *president of the college.*[20]

And so ended the brief stay at Trevecca. Great good, however, was to come out of something which seemed evil. John Wesley had printed some Minutes which had brought about much of the controversy mentioned above, as they were thought by many to contain "dreadful heresies." Mr. Fletcher, on the contrary, felt they contained propositions which ought to be confirmed and so was led to take up his pen in the controversy which followed. This leads us to the second important event which occurred in his life previous to his marriage—the writing of his famous *Checks to Antinomianism,* which are still being printed and distributed two hundred or more years later. His biographer, Joseph Benson, says, "As Mr. Fletcher thought the churches throughout Christendom were verging very fast toward Antinomianism, he judged the propositions contained in those minutes ought rather to be confirmed than revoked."

Readers may wonder, as I did, what Antinomianism really embraces. A definition from an article by Mr. Nicholson in the *Convention Herald* in December, 1973, will enlighten us: "It is the belief of one who holds that to profess faith or belief in Christ frees the one who so believes from the obligations of the moral law."

Wesley considered this belief as an instrument of Satan which strikes directly at the root of all holiness. This heresy practically severs belief in Christ's pardoning grace from the requirements to practice the demands of the moral law. Bishop Cannon gives a clearer picture of the antinomianism which Fletcher was opposing in these words:

> [The Antinomian] is not bound or obliged to do anything which is commanded in the Bible—he need not pray, read the Scripture, feed the poor, obey the moral law, or engage in any exercises which will aid in the promotion of righteousness and purity of life. The whole work of man's salvation was accomplished once for all by Jesus Christ on the cross. Christ's blood and man's sins went away together . . . they trust alone in the imputation of Christ's righteousness.[21]

A few extracts from John Fletcher's letters will best give us his reasons for entering upon such a large enterprise as his *Checks*.

> How much water may at last rush out of a little opening! What are our dear L——'s jealousies come to? Ah, poor college! their conduct and charges of heresy, etc., among other reasons, have stirred me up to write in defense of the Minutes. . . . Methinks I dream, when I reflect I have wrote on controversy! The last subject I thought I should have meddled with. I expect to be roughly handled on the account. Lord, prepare me for this, and everything that may make me cease from man.[22]

Three months later he writes:

> I sent last week a letter of 50 pages upon Antinomianism to the book steward. I beg as upon my bended knees you would revise and correct it, and take off what sounds harsh in point of works (subject), reproof, and style. I have followed my light, which is but that of a smoking flax; put yours to mine. I am charged hereabouts with scattering firebrands, arrows, and death. Quench some of my brands, blunt some of my arrows, and take off all my deaths, except that which I design for Antinomianism.[23]

As he expected, his writing produced sharp criticism. He says in a letter to Mr. Charles Wesley, written about this time, that he "met with loss of friends, and with the charges of novel chimeras on both sides."

Though Mr. Fletcher (like Mr. Wesley) avoided controversy whenever possible, still he could not keep silence when the sacred truths of Scripture were being misinterpreted. Some of the finest explanations of Christ in the Gospels are His refutations of the errors of the Pharisees. To one of his opponents who had written a pamphlet, John Fletcher wrote: "Controversy, though not desirable in itself, yet properly managed, has one hundred times rescued truth groaning under the lash of triumphant error."

Fletcher's humility is very apparent in some of his letters written mostly to his friends about his writings. It is perhaps best seen, however, in his answer to the king, who had been handed a copy of one of his pamphlets. He sent word to the author asking him if he desired preferment in the Church, to which Fletcher replied: "I want nothing but more grace."

The arduous task of writing his *Checks* occupied four or five years of his time, during which he still held his office in Madeley. The controversy began in 1771, and it was not until 1775 that his books were published. His labors took a toll on his already weak body. This necessitated a trip to his own native land in December, 1777. He did little preaching there as he had done on his first trip, but while recuperating he wrote *The Portrait of St. Paul, or The True Model for Christians and Pastors,* in French.

And so we pass on to Mr. Fletcher's marriage—undoubtedly one of the few made in heaven. As a young man Mr. Fletcher had become acquainted with Mary Bosanquet, the latter being only seventeen at the time. Although there was a strong mutual attraction between them, their paths over the next twenty or more years lay in different directions and seldom, if ever, crossed. Occasionally they received news of each other's welfare, and this always tended to confirm the mutual admiration that existed between them. Finally, in July, 1781, Mr. Fletcher visited Miss Bosanquet in her home near Leeds, a step which was quickly followed by a proposal of marriage.

After four months of communication, the way seemed clear for the marriage date to be set. Mary faced many difficulties in the settling of her temporal affairs. In the accompanying sketch of her life we have detailed the way in which all the obstacles vanished before them as they planned for their union. The following is part of a letter written by Sarah Crosby to John Wesley, giving him a detailed account of the circumstances surrounding the wedding.

Monday, November 12 was the day appointed for the outward uniting of those whose hearts were before united by the Holy Spirit. . . . He [Mr. Fletcher] read the Scripture at the top, namely, "Husbands love your wives;" and added, "as Christ loved the Church." Then, turning to us, he said, "My God, what a task! Help me, my friends, by your prayers to fulfil it. As Christ loved the Church! He laid aside His glory for her! He submitted to be born into our world; to be clothed with a human body, subject to all our sinless infirmities. He endured shame, contempt, pain, yea, death itself, for His Church! Oh my God, none is able to fulfil this task without Thine Almighty aid. Help me, Oh my God! Pray for me, Oh my friends."

He next read, "Wives submit yourselves unto your own husbands." Mrs. Fletcher added, "As unto the Lord."

"Well, my dear," returned Mr. Fletcher, "only in the Lord. And if ever I wish you to do anything otherwise, resist me with all your might.". . .

On the Wednesday following, the select society met, and it was a precious season. Among other things, Mr. Fletcher said: "Some of you, perhaps, may be a little surprised at the step my dearest friend and I have taken. But I assure you it was the result of much prayer and mature deliberation. Five and twenty years ago, when I first saw my dear wife, I thought if ever I married, she should be the person. But she was too rich for me to think of, so I banished every thought of the kind. For many years after, I had a distaste to a married life, thinking it impossible to be as much devoted to God in a married, as in a single life. But this objection was removed by reading, 'Enoch begat sons and daughters. And Enoch walked with God, and was not: for God took him.' I then saw that if Enoch, at the head of a family, might walk with God and be fit for translation, our souls, under the Gospel dispensation, might attain the highest degree of holiness in a similar state, if too great an attachment leading the soul from God, rather than to Him, did not take place, instead of that which should be a means of increasing its union with Jesus. Yet still many obstacles stood in my way: but at length they were all removed. Every mountain became a plain, and we are both well assured that the step we have taken has the full approbation of God."[24]

After fourteen months of married life, John Fletcher wrote to Charles Wesley: "I was afraid to say much of the matter, for new married people do not, at first, know each other. But having now lived fourteen months in my new state, I can tell you that Providence has reserved a prize for me, and that my wife is far better to me than the Church to Christ; so that if the parallel fail, it will be on my side."

Mr. Fletcher's marriage had a salutary effect upon the serious consumptive complaint from which he had suffered for so long. With the loving care of his wife, he had a return of his strength as in the days of his youth. Writing to Charles Wesley, he says, "I have yet strength enough to do my parish duty without the help of a curate."

The neglected children of Madeley deeply concerned this man of God, who gave himself daily to instructing about 300 children, eventually building a school in Madeley Wood. In a proposal to the parish he voiced his deep concern thus:

> "Our national depravity turns greatly on these two hinges, the profanation of the Lord's Day, and the neglect of the education of children. Till some way be found of stopping up these two great inlets of wickedness, we must expect to see our workhouses filled with aged parents forsaken by their prodigal children, with wives forsaken by their faithless husbands, and with the wretched offspring of lewd women and drunken men."[25]

There was one outstanding incident in John Fletcher's ministry which illustrates how this man of God could be guided by the Spirit for special circumstances. He tells us about it in his own words:

> One Sunday when I had done reading prayers at Madeley, I went up into the pulpit, intending to preach a sermon which I had prepared

for that purpose. But my mind was so confused that I could not recollect either my text or any part of my sermon. I was afraid I should be obliged to come down without saying anything. But having recollected myself a little, I thought I would say something on the first lesson, which was the third chapter of Daniel, containing the account of the three worthies cast into the fiery furnace. In doing this I found such an extraordinary assistance from God, and such a singular enlargement of heart, that I supposed there must be some peculiar cause for it. I therefore desired, if any of the congregation had met with anything particular, they would acquaint me with it in the ensuing week.

In consequence of this, the Wednesday after, a person came and gave me the following account: Mrs. K. had been for some time much concerned about her soul. She attended the church at all opportunities, and spent much time in private prayer. At this her husband (who is a butcher) was exceedingly enraged, and threatened severely what he would do if she did not leave off going to John Fletcher's church—yea, if she dared to go any more to any religious meetings whatever. When she told him she could not in conscience refrain from going, at least to the parish church, he grew quite outrageous and swore dreadfully that if she went any more he would cut her throat as soon as she came home. This made her cry mightily to God that He would support her in the trying hour. And though she did not feel any great degree of comfort, yet having a sure confidence in God, she determined to go on in her duty and leave the event to Him.

Last Sunday, after many struggles with the devil and her own heart, she came down stairs ready for church. Her husband asked her whether she was resolved to go thither? She told him she was. "Well then," said he, "I shall not, as I intended, cut your throat; but I will heat the oven and throw you into it the moment you come home." Notwithstanding this threatening, which he enforced with many bitter oaths, she went to church, praying all the way that God would strengthen her to suffer whatever might befall her.

While you were speaking of the three Hebrews whom Nebuchadnezzar cast into the burning fiery furnace, she found it all belonged to her, and God applied every word to her heart. And when the sermon was ended, she thought if she had a thousand lives she could lay them all down for God. She felt her whole soul so filled with His love that she hastened home, fully determined to give herself to whatsoever God pleased; nothing doubting but that either He would take her to

Heaven if He suffered her to be burned to death, or that He would some way deliver her even as He did His three servants that trusted in Him.

But when she opened the door, to her astonishment and comfort she found her husband's wrath abated, and soon had reason to believe that he was under a concern for the salvation of his soul. The next Lord's Day, contrary to his former ungodly custom, he attended divine service at the church, and even received the Lord's Supper.[26]

Many dangers surrounded the traveller as he journeyed near and far with the Gospel. These journeys sometimes took him over to Dublin in Ireland and also to outlying towns nearby which called for travel on horse in all kinds of weather. This trusting servant of God at times refused to take remuneration for his labors, deciding rather to have it given to some local need of the poor.

Although his consumptive weakness never found renewal, a fever raged in the area which was to end his ministry. Three weeks before his death he wrote to a friend:

> A week ago I was tried to the quick by a fever with which my dear wife was afflicted: two persons whom she had visited, having been carried off, within a pistol shot of our house, I dreaded her being the third. But the Lord has heard prayer, and she is spared. Oh, what is life! On what a slender thread hang everlasting things! My comfort, however, is that this thread is as strong as the will of God, and the Word of His grace, which cannot be broken.[27]

The happy union of these two godly souls ended with the passing of Mr. Fletcher within three years, nine months, and two days of their wedding day. False rumors of his last days had gotten abroad, and to correct these lies, Mary Fletcher wrote a full report to Mr. Wesley of her husband's closing days and final departure for Heaven. We conclude this sketch with several excerpts from that letter.

> Though but yesterday I parted with my beloved husband's remains, I must now endeavor to collect my wounded mind . . . and give, if possible, some account of the awful (but to him glorious) scene. . . .
>
> On Saturday night his fever first appeared very strong. I begged him not to go to the church in the morning, but let a pious brother who was here preach in the yard. But he told me he believed it was the

will of the Lord, and that he was assured it was right he should go. . . .
As soon as the service was over, we hurried him away to his bed, where
he immediately fainted away. He afterwards dropped into a sleep for
some time, and upon waking, cried out with a pleasant smile, "Now,
my dear, thou seest I am no worse for doing the Lord's work. He never
fails me when I trust in Him.". . . From Sunday his strength decreased
amazingly. . . .

On Wednesday, after groaning all day as it were under the weight
of the power of God, he told me he had received such a manifestation
of the full meaning of that word, "God is love," as he could never be
able to tell. "It fills me," said he; "it fills me every moment. Oh Polly!
my dear Polly! God is love! Shout, shout aloud! Oh! it so fills me, I
want a gust of praise to go to the ends of the earth.". . .

On Thursday his speech began to fail. . . . On Saturday afternoon his fever seemed quite off. . . . In the evening his fever returned with violence, and the mucus falling on the windpipe occasioned him to be almost strangled. He suffered greatly, and it was
feared the same painful emotion would continue and grow more
violent to the last. This I felt most exquisitely, and cried to the
Lord to remove it. And, glory be to His Name, He did remove it;
and it returned no more in that way.

As night drew on, I thought I perceived him dying very fast. His
fingers could now hardly move to make the sign (which he seemed
scarce ever to forget), and his speech, as it seemed, was quite gone. I
said, "My dear creature, I ask not for myself, I know thy soul; but, for
the sake of others, if Jesus is very present with thee, lift thy right hand."
He did so. I added, "If the prospect of glory sweetly opens before thee,
repeat the sign." He then raised it again—and, in half a minute, a
second time. Then he threw it up with all his remaining strength, as if
he would reach the top of the bed!

After this his dear hands moved no more; but on my saying, "Art
thou in much pain?" he answered, "No." From this time he entered
into a state that might be called a kind of sleep, though with eyes open
and fixed, and his hands utterly void of any motion. For the most part
he sat upright against pillows, with his head a little inclined to one
side, and so remarkably composed and triumphant was his countenance
that the least trace of death was scarcely discernible in it.

Twenty-four hours my dearly beloved was in this situation, breath-
ing like a person in common sleep. About thirty-five minutes past ten, on

Sunday night, August 14th, his precious soul entered into the joy of the Lord, without one struggle or groan, in the fifty-sixth year of his age.

Often he had said, when hearing of happy deaths, "Well, let us get holy lives, and we will leave the rest to God." But I, who was scarce a minute at a time from him night or day, can truly say that there was the strongest reason to believe

"No cloud did arise, to darken the skies,
Or hide for one moment his Lord from his eyes."[28]

The Old Vicarage at Madeley

John Fletcher's Tomb outside Madeley Church

Mary Fletcher
1739-1815

Laytonstone Hall, Essex
Birthplace of Mary (Bosanquet) Fletcher

Mary Fletcher

W HEN God designs to confer a great blessing, He frequently puts a sentence of death on the means that seem to
lead thereto—as in the case of Abraham and Sarah."[1] This obser-
vation was made by a Mr. Bridges, and was a means of blessing to
Mary Bosanquet when she found herself at forty-two years of age
in a financial dilemma. But Mary was just on the brink of a change
of plan for her entire after-life which was to usher her into a place
of usefulness beyond anything she could have contemplated.

First, however, all she had trusted in had to be stripped and
her soul severely tested in the furnace of God's appointing. But we
must go back over some years in order to understand God's purpose in the life of this dedicated woman of God.

Mary Bosanquet was born into an affluent home in
Laytonstone Hall, Essex, England, on September 12, 1739. From
a very small child she had an unusual hunger to know God. At ten
years of age this hunger was intensified as she came into contact
with some godly women in Methodism, one of whom was a servant employed in their home. The worldliness and pleasures enjoyed by her family she could no longer appreciate. Abel Stevens,
a Methodist historian, writing of this period says:

> Her parents wished her to accompany them to Scarborough, hop-
> ing to dispel her religious thoughtfulness by the summer gaieties. But
> with filial affectionateness and Christian meekness she pleaded to be
> spared what she deemed so great a peril. She was left with her friends in
> London, where she now became acquainted with Sarah Ryan, a woman
> of remarkable character, one of John Wesley's correspondents, who had
> been housekeeper at his Kingswood school.

At her house, Mary Bosanquet found the companionship her devout heart needed. "The more I saw of this family," she says, "the more I was convinced Christ had yet a pure church below. Often, while in their company, I thought myself with the hundred and twenty that waited to be baptized by the Holy Spirit. Whenever I was from home this was the place of my residence, and truly I found it to be a little Bethel."[2]

Less and less did this young teenager feel attracted to the gaieties of Bath and London. At twenty-one years of age, a conversation with her father brought an abrupt end to Mary's sojourn in her own family. We have the account in her own words:

> One day my father said to me, "There is a particular promise which I require of you: that you will never, on any occasion, either now or hereafter, attempt to make your brothers what you call a Christian."
>
> I answered (looking to the Lord), "I think, Sir, I dare not consent to that."
>
> He replied, "Then you force me to put you out of my house."
>
> I answered, "Yes, Sir, according to your views of things, I acknowledge it; and if I may but have your approval, no situation will be disagreeable."[3]

Accompanied by a servant girl, Mary moved from a home of plenty to take up residence in a two room apartment in Hoxton, near London, where her furnishings were Spartan indeed. This was to be her first experience in enduring God's stripping process. But those proved days of blessing to which she looked back with joy in later years.

Mary's financial position, however, was most secure, for she was not without funds. Her grandparents had left her a legacy as well as large premises at Laytonstone Hall. She moved there on May 24, 1763, and found ample opportunity to gather the orphan, the destitute, and the ill under her roof. Here she stayed for five years and then was advised to take a farm in order to better supply those under her care with milk and other farm products. So in 1768 she took a farm in Yorkshire called Cross Hall.

A gentleman with a family of five was taken into her household, the man taking oversight of her farm. However, after seven years it was apparent that mismanagement was beginning to place the farm in financial straits. Following advice from mature counselors, Mary decided to continue another seven years in which time, she was told, the farm would begin to become a sound investment. Doubtless there were some who took advantage at this time of this benevolent, godly heiress, knowing that she was without a husband or family member who would understand her situation and give spiritual advice.

Mary's fortunes, however, were to take a right about change and her spiritual coast of usefulness enlarged. But it was not through pleasant circumstances that this was to be accomplished, and it had to be preceded by her second stripping. She faced bankruptcy and perhaps even imprisonment and, at the worst, a lifetime of spending her legacy in merely paying the interest on her debt. It was indeed a testing time, and the furnace heat was at times unbearable. In a diary entry on January 13th, 1781, she expresses her dilemma:

> I have a most narrow path to walk in! I am called to live by faith, indeed. As I was at prayer this morning, I was led to ask of the Lord that He would bring me out of all my difficulties in His own way. Certainly the whole earth is the Lord's, and I asked of Him such a situation in life as will most glorify Himself.
>
> It was brought before me, "Perhaps that will be by bringing you to entire poverty."
>
> I asked my heart, "Am I willing on that condition to be made holy?" And I felt I could say, "Yes, Lord, yes."
>
> Again, the thought was suggested, "But perhaps to a parish-house, while your income goes each year for your debts?"
>
> I answered, "Thy will be done!" It was then represented as if I was on a common-side, dying destitute of every human help or comfort. In that I felt great sweetness. But the sorest stroke was still behind: "What if you should die in debt and leave nothing to pay, and so through you the Gospel be reproached?"

This came the nearest of all. But it was clearly shown me that the fear of the Gospel being blamed often arose from our fear of personal reproach; for as to the truths of God, He would take care of them. And if I was really wrong, it would be for the glory of God to have it made manifest; and if He was but glorified, my soul was content.

Certainly, thought I, if it was in my power to break off my expenses, it would be right so to do; and I do right in contriving every way I can towards it. But as all my endeavors are always frustrated, I see no way but to cast myself on the will of God and embrace, as His will, poverty and deep reproach; and still continue to believe in His promises, till I see, even by the time of my death, that there has not been an accomplishment of them. Perhaps, after all, I am right. Perhaps the day will come (impossible as it now appears) when I shall "have plenty of silver," and then the light shall indeed shine on my way.

Next June I shall have been fourteen years from Laytonstone, and the September following I shall be forty-two years old. It may be that soon after that time deliverance may appear. The words rested on my mind, "By the way that thou wentest, by that way shalt thou return." Lord, Thou knowest what they mean; but I see all sorts of crucifixions are needful for me. Oh my hard heart! What need hath it had of breaking![4]

Seventeen years later she recalls this time of stripping. She could have said with Job, "Truly he hath stripped me of my glory."

At twenty-four I had a plentiful fortune, but all seemed lost. Yet God said in my heart, "Thou shalt lend and not borrow." I was, however, at that time borrowing of many, my own money being in estates. I feared I should not at last pay all. Therefore, for fear of deception, I spoke freely to several of my losses, and especially to those whose money I had on interest. Many said, "Depend upon it, she is not worth ten pounds, for everyone makes the best they can of their affairs."

Such a sentence of death seemed to come over all my worldly affairs! And yet, when God's time came, how did it all turn about! Now, it may be asked, "Why does God take this way?" Mr. Bridges gives a sweet answer: "God gives His blessings in that manner that shall most show that 'He is God.'"

Now had my fortune remained unlessened, as it came from my parents, I should not have so clearly seen the hand of God. But, like

Joseph, we must sometimes be sold into Egypt in order to have our promises fulfilled—of becoming the "sheaf lifted up." Of late I have feared lest I should look to my plenty more than I ought and not live by faith.[5]

There was a fleshly way out open to Mary at this time which would have avoided the appearance of seeming failure on all her ventures. A neighboring Christian farmer who had been widowed had endeavored for some years to repeatedly entice Mary into marriage, promising at the same time to assume her indebtedness. We see the sagacity and thoughtfulness of this forty-two year old woman, for she realized that she had not the profound respect for this suitor that could call forth a serious vow to obey him. But there was another reason for her decision to refuse this tempting offer. When only seventeen years of age, Mary had met John Fletcher. There had been a mutual attraction, but the Swiss Vicar of Madeley did not feel that his income was sufficient to make him a suitable husband for the young heiress.

For fifteen years they had not even seen one another, and rumor had it that Rev. Fletcher's four years of residence in Switzerland for health reasons would lengthen into a permanent stay. Surely Mary's every avenue of escape seemed doomed. However, the fifty-two year old vicar did return, and on hearing of Mary's bankrupt condition, felt all his scruples were removed. He made no delay in going to Cross Hall and approaching her. She accepted the proposal. Providence swiftly began to favor her. She had been told that Cross Hall Farm would bring a very small sum which would not begin to pay off the debt, but within a day or two someone offered almost three times the amount originally suggested. In another few days, someone else offered money for the cattle, thus reducing Mary's indebtedness to one hundred pounds. A brother of hers, not knowing of her need, unexpectedly sent exactly one hundred pounds, and within days what had appeared inescapable ruin turned to blessing.

These two middle-aged people, after waiting twenty-five years, soon set the wedding date. Former sorrows were forgotten in the wonderful fellowship and love between these two holy persons. Fletcher once said that their marriage was one of the few made in Heaven. A year before her widowhood, Mary's cup of happiness was running over.

> I have the best of husbands, who daily grows more and more spiritual, and I think more healthful, being far better than when we first married. My call is also so clear, and I have such liberty in the work and such sweet encouragement among the people.[6]
>
> For a good while past, my dear husband has joined with me in prayer in an uncommon manner. We are led to offer ourselves to do and suffer all the will of God. Something seems to tell me I must have more of the bitter cup, and these words are much with me, "that ye may be able to withstand in the evil day, and having done all, to stand."[7]

However, they did not allow anything to interfere with God's call, and as Mr. Fletcher was called on now and again to journey into other parts in order to minister, Mary felt that the language of her heart was:

> Happy to meet, yet free to part,
> Through Thee forever one in heart.

In a letter to Mr. Wesley, Mary spoke of their time together:

> For some time before his last illness, his precious soul (always alive to God) was particularly penetrated by the nearness of eternity. There was scarce an hour in which he was not calling upon me to drop every thought and every care that we might attend to nothing but drinking deeper into God. We spent much time in wrestling prayer for the fullness of the Spirit and were led in a very particular manner to an act of abandonment of our whole selves into the hands of God, to do or to suffer whatever was pleasing to Him. Our union increased daily. . . . We had a little paradise together.[8]

Little had the happy newly weds realized, as they stood on the threshold of their future, that three years, nine months, and two days would be all the time that would be given to them to share their happiness. Within a few months of reaching the peak of marital bliss, Mary found herself penning these lines:

> When I wrote last (July 26), I was indeed arrived at the summit of human felicity. My cup did indeed run over. I often said, "Lord, how is this? Am I indeed one of those of whom it is said, 'These are they who came out of great tribulation'? My way is strewed with roses. I am ready to say with Joseph 'The Lord hath made me to forget all my afflictions and all my father's house.'"
>
> But Oh! how shall I write it? On the 14th August, 1785, the dreadful moment came! The sun of my earthly joys forever set, and the cloud arose which casts the sable on all my future life! . . .
>
> I am truly a desolate woman who hath no helper but Thee. I remember a little before the translation of my dearest love, we were drawn out continually to ask for a greater measure of the Spirit—such a measure as was given at Pentecost, or, in other words, such a manifestation of the loving nature of God as should fulfill in us that promise, "Ye are the temples of the Holy Ghost." This I asked and pleaded for, and that on any condition. My dear Mr. Fletcher used to say, "That is right, Polly. Let us hold fast there and leave all the rest to God, though He should be constrained to part us asunder to give the answer."[9]

Mary Fletcher, however, was a woman who sought to understand God's ways. A little over a year after this terrible blow which stripped her of life's greatest joy she could say,

> This day has also been a time of deep examination. What difference do I find between this and the last fourteenth of August, the day of my dear husband's death? I find a good deal, many ways.
>
> First, I have more vehement longing after Christ.
>
> Secondly, I am stripped of all desire of human comforts, and dead to earth in a fuller degree than I was before in any part of my life.
>
> Thirdly, that fierce conflict of temptation which I endured at that time has wrought for my good.
>
> Fourthly, I am more constant and faithful in private prayer; indeed it is my one business. I have a more watchful spirit.
>
> Fifthly, I feel a more perfect resignation; and though my wound continually bleeds, yet I can continually say, "Thy will be done." Yet

nothing can supply the place of the full indwelling Spirit. The Lord is ever with me. I have surprising helps and deliverances and victory in every trial. I feel I am crucified to the world; but yet I want "the promise of the Father" in its fullness.[10]

On the third anniversary of her husband's death she writes, "Three years I have now passed in solemn, awful widowhood, but glory be to my God, I have found it to be three years of prayer. Never did I know three years of such suffering, and never did I know three years of such prayer."

Again, looking back, she says, "I was the happiest of women. I had everything which friendship, the most heavenly and refined, could give. My helps were too many; I could not feel my deep nothingness. God has stripped me of all! Yet I will look every moment for the complete victory."

God was indeed enlarging her. She notes that Philip Doddridge had said, "There must be an enlargement of soul before any remarkable success on others; and a great diligence in prayer and strict watchfulness over my own soul previous to any remarkable and habitual enlargement in my ministry; and deep humiliation must precede both."

It is most remarkable to note how God would use this prepared vessel in Madeley. Mr. Fletcher had once said to his wife, "My dear, when you marry me, you must marry my parish." This union of the shepherd with the sheep of Madeley was to continue in a rich manner for thirty more years. Her husband had wished her to remain at Madeley, and she faithfully performed his wish. She tells in her diary how this was made possible.

I received a message from Mr. Kennerson, letting me know that I should never be turned out of the house but might rent it; which I received as an answer from the Lord directing my way. . . . The Lord also answered my dear husband's prayer with regard to the work of the Lord beyond all expectation. When he repeatedly expressed his desire that I should stay here, I replied, "Oh how can I bear the place without thee? How can I bear to stay and see perhaps a carnal ministry?"

He answered, "Thou dost not know what God may do. Perhaps there may never be a carnal ministry here." And so it proved. The Rev. Mr. Gilpin and his wife, being on the spot, were at that season kind and tender friends to me; and Mr. Kennerson desired him to supply the church till he should return to his own living, which was not for some months. The Lord then provided for us a precious young man, Mr. Melvill Horne, who had traveled some time in connection with Mr. Wesley; and concerning whom my dear Mr. Fletcher had (before his illness) expressed a desire that he might be his successor.[11]

The manse in which they had lived she rented for thirty more years. She was given the right to help choose any succeeding vicar, and this she did with great success. Thus she was enabled to carry on a ministry after her husband's death that would still combine Church of England members with the Methodist societies. The vicars were usually those who were sympathetic to the Methodist cause.

Another favorable providence was that Mr. Wesley, usually most reticent towards assenting to a woman's ministry, felt that Mary Fletcher enjoyed an unusual share of God's blessing. He therefore gave her his blessing to minister as much as seven or eight times a week to the combined societies in Madeley and Madeley Wood.

That it was God's plan for her to remain at Madeley was made very apparent to her, for she writes in her diary the proofs of this being God's call:

My dear Mr. Fletcher always said that if he died he believed that I was to stay here; and there are some circumstances which reconciled me so to do:

1. I was never in any situation in which I had so much opportunity of doing good as in this place; and that in various ways, public and private; and to many that live at a distance also. These are providentially thrown in my way, and I find such clear leadings of the Spirit in conversing with them that I am constrained to say, "If I choose for the work of God, here I must abide and fix my home."

2. Here I have a great many sweet, lively souls to converse with. My meetings are more satisfactory to myself than in any place I ever

yet was in, and I still feel it suited to me as a soil in which my soul grows.

3. It suits my temporal affairs, this house being cheap, and several other circumstances are also advantageous.

4. I never found any other part agree as well with my health as this has done. From a child, I never could live in London nor in any close place. Here I have had better health than ever before; only at this season I find the waves of sorrow have thrown me some paces nearer my eternal Home. . . .[12]

I am amazed at the goodness of the Lord in many things. I see Him opening all my way before me, day by day. He cuts out my work and shows me how to employ every hour.[13]

In her sixtieth year, Mrs. Fletcher was to experience a further stripping. When she was in her twenties, she had taken an orphan of four years of age into her home. Sally Lawrence had grown up as her own child and had become most useful to her in every way. Now it seemed that she was to be taken from her. The following diary entries reveal her deep attachment to Sally and her deep sorrow at the prospect of losing her:

Oh teach me "the way of faith more perfectly!" My dear child grows worse. She coughs almost continually. I feel it as a knife in my heart. She is my earthly all, and in the whole universe there is but one thing I love more than her, that is, "the will of my God." To that I do, I must, I will refer in everything! . . .

My dear child is kept in much peace, and she prays that the trial may answer all that the Lord intends before it is removed. Lord, I add my prayers to hers: so let it be! I shall certainly feel her loss severely. With her I can consult about every circumstance; to her I can tell every temptation; and her watchful attention over each infirmity of my body is uncommon. Her skill in managing all the affairs of my family is very great. She takes off all burdens from me and leaves me wholly free.

Her help in the work of God also is unspeakable. She assists in memory, in speaking to the people, in judging concerning them, in reproving and exhorting. I do nothing in the church affairs but with her counsel. In her own meetings, a few of which she will keep up, her word is clothed with power, and many, very many, are weeping through fear of her loss. I feel the Lord requires me to keep looking to Him alone and living only the present hour with a continual Abraham-like spirit, holding my sacrifice before the Lord to Whom my more than all is due.[14]

"I am a woman of a sorrowful spirit." My dear child grows worse. Well, I will cling to that rock, "Thy will be done." This shall be my momentary employ the remainder of my life. Not one on earth with whom I can converse of the past trials through which she hath walked with me! Well, my Lord, Thou knowest my solitary situation. The pains she suffers from that dreadful cough, and a complication of complaints, would constrain, I think, any besides herself to keep their bed. But while there is a grain of strength given to her, she will use it, both in the work of God, and in the care of our affairs. I will hang on that word, "I will bring the blind by a way that they knew not. I will lead them in paths which they have not known."[15]

On December 3rd my dearest child and friend went triumphantly to glory! . . . How does the Lord help us in the needful hour! In the ordering of her funeral and various things which fell on me alone, I have been brought through, and proved her dying words, "He will put His everlasting arms underneath you." He doth, and I am borne up. But Oh, what a loss do I sustain! God alone knows what she was to me, and Himself alone can fill the aching void![16]

Mary's spiritual hunger for more of God increased daily. I have never read a woman's diary that was more spiritual. Little details of household management, entertainment of visitors, or household repairs—these are not the subject of her daily diary writings. Her prayer life increased: she would stop seven times a day to pray. Day after day, all through the years, she repeats the deep longing in her heart for a more complete conformity to God, a deeper union with Himself:

I know I do taste of pure love, but I do not abide in Jesus; therefore I do not bring forth "much fruit." There is an entering in to rest which I have been particularly led of late to ask for. Sometimes it seems near, and I am waiting for it in a clearer manner than usual.[17]

Oh how sweet is the communion of saints when we meet with those who are all alive, or who are thirsting so to be! But alas, how rarely are they found![18]

I feel my soul does come forward. Constancy in early rising is a great blessing to me both as a Christian and as a mistress.[19]

I have of late been much tried with such a stupor on me in the morning that I cannot rise till near seven o'clock. This pains me much. Lord, make me more active in Thy work! I have since observed some answer to prayer with regard to rising in the morning.[20]

I knew well that "all the good done upon the earth is the Lord's doing," and He can work by the meanest instrument. However, this was the conclusion: I must ask and wrestle for every meeting, public and private, and hang by faith on Christ alone, believing that word, "It is not you that speak, but the Spirit of your Father which speaketh in you." . . . I can do nothing without much prayer.[21]

I found freedom in prayer, so that an hour on my knees seemed to pass as quickly as a quarter usually does.[22]

The Spirit of God is a spirit of illumination. That I, in a low degree, feel. I have a light which increases in reading the Scriptures, and some fresh views of the amazing glory of redemption are given to me.

Secondly, the Spirit of God is the spirit of prayer, of groans unutterable. A little of this I feel; but out of seven times a day in prayer, often I have not what I call the "spirit of prayer" above three or four times.

Thirdly, the Spirit of God is a spirit of humiliation. Surely I may say I have this mark; but I do not love humiliation, at least till I have time to reflect. I do not run to embrace it nor pick it up as I would a jewel.

Fourthly, the Spirit of God is a spirit of sanctification, purifying the heart. I do feel it is working that in me. Yet I am not free from reptile thoughts—those which crawl on the earth. They do not, it is true, carry the stamp of sin upon them, yet they hinder prayer.

Fifthly, the Spirit of God is a spirit of love. What shall I say to this? My love to God does increase. I can say "Oh God, my chief joy!" But

I can very seldom say, "Oh God, my exceeding joy!"[23]

Her views of the awfulness of sin increased as she matured. Looking back at her experience at twenty-one while at Hoxton, she says,

> That salvation I experienced at Hoxton was certainly a drop from the living fountain; but I had not then a full discovery of sin. Since that time, Oh what a depth of iniquity, what huge mountains of ingratitude have I mourned over! I once thought I could not sit down on the level with the greatest outward sinners. . . . The sight I have had of inbred sin; the base departure of my heart from a close walk with God; and the depth of self and pride I have there discovered is, in my eyes, more dreadful than outward transgression.[24]

> Am I deeply conscious that the root of all sin is in having lost God and found self in His place? And do I continually see holiness to consist in the being sunk in my own nothingness that God alone may be exalted in my soul?[25]

> I was thinking today, "What is sin?" It is a turning out of the presence of God and departing from union with Him; drawing back from the attraction. While that is kept up no sin is imputed. Many blunders may be made; but while the heart keeps attached to Jesus, cleaving to Him by faith, these words stand good, "There is no condemnation to them which are in Christ Jesus." The will being still fastened to His cross, all that is wanting is a closer attention to the Spirit. Then these blunders would be rectified. My one concern must be to keep in the presence of God, lying before Him as clay, and He will do all His will in me.[26]

This deeper view of sin made her very conscious of any imperfection in her walk. She constantly strove to watch her conversation and felt at times that she sinned through speaking too quickly.

> I ask power to consecrate the faculty of speech to the service of my God, so that I may never again speak an unadvised word.[27]

> My grief lies here. I am condemned, often once or twice a day, for

some word or thought or action—chiefly in words. Indeed, the condemnation does not seem to be from the Lord, as if it would come between my soul and Him; but I see I have spoken unadvisedly with my lips, and I cannot bear the horror of the view.

There are some persons with whom I have much business to transact who do not see alike or cordially love one another. In some things both are right, in others both are wrong. I have this connection at present two ways—personally and by correspondence. I find it a hard thing to bear my testimony against that which is wrong and to approve that which is right in both, and yet neither to write nor speak but exactly so far as truth and love require. Oh that I may from this day see as in letters of blood before my eyes continually those words of the apostle, "He that offendeth not in tongue, the same is a perfect man, able also to bridle the whole body." Ah, Lord! how far am I yet from this perfection![28]

Later she says, "Oh how hard never to offend with the tongue! As to my outward walk: have I watched over my tongue? David says in Psalm 69, 'I will take heed to my ways that I sin not with my tongue. I will keep my mouth with a bridle while the wicked is before me.'"

God gave wonderful harmony in Madeley during those thirty years which followed her husband's death, and it was only during the last year of her life that she found that the Church of England Vicar objected to combining the work at the Church with the Methodist Societies. We see here the hand of God so marvelously working on her behalf.

We omit the latter years of this saintly woman's life because they have been detailed in our book, *Old Age—Handicap or Blessing?* which is part of the "Call Back" series. We are also reprinting the unabridged edition of Mrs. Fletcher's full biography and diary so that any one who has been inspired through reading this brief sketch might have in detail a history of her growth in grace and be inspired by her unending thirst after more of God.

We close with a tribute from Abel Stevens, the historian:

With a piety as fervid as that of any canonized woman of Romanism, she combined the accomplishments of a refined education which protected her from the perils of mysticism, and a habit of practical usefulness which crowned her long life with labors and charities.

An author who belonged not to Methodism has said of her that "in the apostolic age she would have been a Priscilla and have taken her rank among the presbyteresses or lady confessors of the primitive church. Had she been born within the Romish communion, she probably would have been enrolled among the saints of the calendar."[29]

Cross Hall, home of Mary Bosanquet

John Frederick Oberlin
1740-1826

John Frederick Oberlin

THE isolated community of Ban de la Roche desperately needed a pastor. It could be truly said that there were sheep scattered "on every high hill and mountain" who needed a shepherd. Nestled in the heart of the Vosges Mountains of Eastern France, where the icy grasps of winter held the inhabitants bound for six months of the year, this poverty-stricken parish did not present an inviting proposition to any aspiring young minister. Then, as now, for the heart of man has not changed over the centuries, shepherds were plentiful in the prosperous cities, the warm valleys, and the comfortable parsonages. What educated young man would invest his life where the terrain was so rugged that roads were practically non-existent? Who would choose such a secluded life made necessary by the extreme poverty and ignorance of the people, or who would voluntarily forego the refinements and financial inducements of city living?

M. Stouber, a German Lutheran minister, had doubtless asked himself the same questions. He had pastored these scattered sheep for some years and had made some inroads on the hopeless condition of the population. He would have doubtless remained with his flock for a life-time had it not been that the health of his dying wife demanded that he live in a friendlier clime than that of the Vosges Mountains. But where was he to find a successor who would naturally care for these sheep?

D. L. Moody once said that the world had yet to see what God could do with one who was wholly consecrated to Himself. Perhaps Mr. Moody had never heard of John Frederick Oberlin

whom God called in his youth to a life of self-sacrifice and courageous endeavor, or of the vow which he wrote at twenty years of
age after being influenced by the life of Philip Doddridge. The
following is but a portion of his covenant, which Frederick renewed ten years later:

> In the name of the Lord of Hosts, I this day renounce all former
> lords that have had dominion over me—the joys of the world in which
> I have too much delighted and all carnal desires. I renounce all perish-
> able things in order that God may constitute my all. I consecrate to
> Thee all that I am and all that I have; the faculties of my mind, the
> members of my body, my fortune, and my time. Grant me grace, Oh
> Father of mercies, to employ all to Thy glory and in obedience to Thy
> commands for ardently and humbly I desire to be Thine through the
> endless ages of eternity.
>
> Shouldest Thou be pleased to make me in this life the instrument
> in leading others to Thee, give me strength and courage openly to de-
> clare Thy service and to persuade my brethren to dedicate themselves
> to it also.

M. Stouber had heard much of the piety and devotion of
Oberlin and determined to search him out. He may well have had
strong misgivings as he considered presenting the need of his parish to this twenty-six year old doctor of divinity who could com-
mand any post in Strasbourg. But perhaps he had also heard how
this same young man had refused several calls to churches, because he had felt that the living was too comfortable and that he
was not yet ready to take up pastoral life.

Philip was led by the Holy Spirit to leave a revival scene in a
city and go "desert way" just for one man—the Ethiopian eunuch.
Stouber had not been sent on a less important mission. A modern
enactment of the Book of Acts was about to transpire when he
climbed the three flights of stairs to Oberlin's attic apartment. It is
very possible that M. Stouber was not prepared for what he found
upon entering the sparsely furnished room. On a bed surrounded
by paper curtains lay Frederick Oberlin, nursing a badly infected
tooth. A more sophisticated visitor might have been discouraged

by these conditions but Stouber, without more ado, acquainted the young man with the object of his call. Then, noticing a pan hanging from the ceiling he asked, "What is the purpose of that pan?" Oberlin explained that his mother prepared the main meal of the day and, in addition, would give him a piece of bread to take to his attic. He would place this bread in a pan, add salt and water, and have it for his evening meal which he highly relished.

This Spartan living doubtless impressed the visitor, but, had he known that Frederick placed two logs in his bed every evening in order to make early morning rising less difficult, M. Stouber would have been even more impressed. Or had he been told that, as a child, Oberlin would save his pocket money and give it to the needy whom he met in the market or on the street, M. Stouber would have been convinced that he had found his man.

Oberlin, on his part, had a question for his visitor. Why was Stouber leaving his post if it was such a needy spot? When told that Mrs. Stouber was dying and needed a change of climate, he was soon satisfied. But a difficulty still stood in his way. Not long before, he had taken the post of chaplain for a military academy. How could he fail to fulfill his commission there? When, however, Stouber suggested that he return the next day to receive a reply, Oberlin felt it unnecessary, for he had already made up his mind to accept the invitation if he could obtain a discharge from his recent commission.

It is most interesting to trace God's hand in the preparation of the man God chose to pastor those needy sheep in Ban de la Roche, an isolated, rocky mountain patch of 9,000 acres, containing five villages and perhaps one hundred families. Oberlin's birth, his training, and daily choice of self-discipline had all fitted him, unknown to himself, for almost sixty years of labor in this neglected part of France.

In a letter written in later years to his parish, Oberlin went over his past life and how he had been sent to labor among them. He says, "God, after having trained and prepared me from my youth, sent me to thee that I might be useful. He alone is wise, good, almighty, and merciful and as for me, I am but a poor, feeble, wretched man."

John Frederick Oberlin had indeed been blessed with a godly heritage. He was born in Strasbourg on August 31, 1740. Both his parents took time with their nine children for the father, being a teacher, was well fitted to tutor his own family. Every Thursday, he would drill his seven boys at his country residence, and would march ahead, beating a drum and giving out orders to them in order to teach them military discipline. His mother, a God-fearing and cultured woman, would read each night to them out of some book after which the nine children would beg for a hymn. Then would come the prayer which would always close their day. Perhaps it is not surprising that Oberlin felt the drawings of the unseen God even as a small child and would pray Samuel's prayer, "Speak Lord, for Thy servant heareth."

Although the father had difficulty in managing his large household on his teacher's stipend, he nevertheless allowed each child some pocket money so that they could indulge themselves in candy, cake, or fruit. But Frederick never used his money thus, but would store it up in a tin box. When bills in the family could not be met, he would run for his little box and empty it out to supply the need at hand. The poor and destitute were also the recipients of his meager savings. In his unbounded generosity, we can see the grown man in the small boy, and understand better his life of unstinting giving.

Frederick Oberlin graduated at eighteen with a bachelor's degree and five years later he received his doctorate. When he was twenty-six years of age, he met Stouber on that memorable occasion and subsequently embarked upon his life's calling.

Picture, if you can, two lonely figures trudging up the mountain path to Waldbach, for Mrs. Oberlin had decided to accompany her son to his new home where M. Stouber and his wife had previously lived. The accompanying picture was sketched by a visi-

Oberlin's Residence at Waldbach

tor to this mountain dwelling which was to be Frederick's home for many years to come.

Motherly solicitude for her son in his isolated post caused Mrs. Oberlin to prevail upon Fritz to seek a partner in life, and he agreed to leave the choice to her. She sought out two seemingly eligible women from wealthy backgrounds and introduced them to her son. God, in his own providence, allowed both attempts at match-making to prove abortive, for He had chosen otherwise for Oberlin, someone who was to prove indeed a worthy woman for the dedicated pastor.

Realizing Frederick's need of a housekeeper, Sophia Oberlin left social life in Strasbourg for the solitude of her brother's home in the mountains. It was then that a providential happening changed all John's future. Sophia, upon discovering that a cousin of theirs was ill, suggested she visit them in Waldbach, hoping that the mountain air would restore her to health. And so young and fashionable Madeline Witter came to their mountain retreat and soon improved rapidly under Sophia's loving care.

Madeline's father was a man of means, and her mother was the daughter of a university lecturer. Oberlin was suspicious of this witty and fascinating girl and considered her a worldly intruder. For several Sabbaths, he denounced from the pulpit the spirit of the world in professed Christians, thus hoping to convict his fashionable cousin. His reproofs were not limited to the pulpit, but Madeline's quick repartee and sound sense in conversation unconsciously captured the heart of the young minister. Before the time came to bid her good-bye, God had indicated to Oberlin that she was to be his companion in this sterile and desolate region. Surprisingly enough, Madeline consented to be his wife, and so for sixteen years of marriage she entered into his parish work with zest and interest. The tremendous needs all about her gave her ample opportunity to use the rich talents her heavenly Father had given her.

Seven children were added to the household, four boys and three girls, who were soon put to work for the villagers. The Oberlin home was unusual in many respects. A text of Scripture hung over each of the many doors of Waldbach. Maps, information concerning biology and scientific research also adorned the walls and doors. But above all, God reigned in this well-ordered household.

There was much for the young couple to do in the new pastorate. The establishment of educational privileges for the children was one of their first attempts at reform. Iron-willed adults, suspicious of their youthful pastor, rigorously opposed the building of the first schoolhouse. Already taxed heavily, the inhabitants of this lonely mountain region resented any improvement that might suggest an increase in taxation, or the adding of any other burden to their already burdensome lives.

It was not until the zealous young minister promised to undertake the financial burden of the entire enterprise, that the building finally became a possibility even though the ensuing cost was equivalent to his salary for one year. Although it took several years to clear the debt, Oberlin undertook the construction of a second school in a neighboring village with the same financial burden resting on his shoulders. The people, however, became convinced of the advantages of such enterprises and from then on, took upon themselves the responsibility for the erection of further schools.

It was not only education, however, which needed improvement in Ban de la Roche. Oberlin realized there were few roads or bridges in the Vosges to link even the scattered villages, let alone make contact possible with the outer world. He felt keenly that doctors, medicine, and emergency supplies must be made more easily accessible. He also realized that produce had no ready market because of the difficulty of transport. However, when he turned his attention to this great need he found that road and bridge-making projects met with an unfavorable response from his people. A plot to waylay the road-builder was met with such fearless candor that, at last, two hundred men followed their minister with pick axes, ready to break the large stones which blasting had brought down the mountain sides.

When it came to agriculture, Oberlin coped with the primitive conditions of his parish with the same ingenuity. He knew that new strains of fruit trees and new seed potatoes would greatly benefit the villagers, who would often take their fruit from wild trees which but meagerly supplied their wants. Very wisely though unobtrusively, Oberlin had planted fruit trees on both sides of their main thoroughfare, and the villagers would watch with interest the orchard mature and acknowledge that the yields far exceeded any other in those valleys. This convinced them that their pastor's method was worth trying, so they eventually became willing to use imported fruit trees and seeds.

Oberlin also taught them how to turn every bit of kitchen refuse into compost, and thus enrich the impoverished soil. The children would shred old cloth and shoes for composting and were repaid for their diligence. Soon the mountain terrain began to blossom.

Thus the faithful pastor tried to provide for every need of his beloved parishioners. He was known to have spent an entire night traveling to Strasbourg for medicine for a sick patient. When he realized that his brief knowledge of medicine was being taxed to the limit, he chose a young man to be trained to minister to the sick. Eventually his son John was likewise trained, but the arduous work of doctoring in such precarious places and in all weathers, meant his early death.

It was little wonder that Oberlin's predecessor looked on these reforms with some suspicion. Good it was for the young man to have had such a spiritual advisor to see that his philanthropy did not exceed his spiritual resources. Listen to the admonishing letter written by Stouber:

> I must remind you that even when deeply engaged in good works, it is possible to depart from spiritual Christianity; and I would, on this account, urge you to maintain a constant guard over yourself. You have been brought under the influence of religion, and in the usual sense of the term converted to God. But, without constant prayer to Him, and

the most zealous watchfulness, there is a danger lest you should rest satisfied with this, and relapse into indifference. By being so incessantly occupied in the prosecution of your favorite schemes, and destitute of stimulating society, you may become cold and lukewarm in your religious duties, and less devoted in your service to God, even though busily employed in promoting the well-being of your fellow-creatures. . . .

I have sometimes discerned with deep concern the danger incident to young persons; coldness and lukewarmness after the first fervor of religious feeling has subsided; self sufficiency in what they have effected, and too great tendency in absorption of mind in even laudable and benevolent pursuits.

There are two things to which I particularly wish to direct your attention—prayer and the Holy Scriptures. I find it necessary in order to keep up habitual communion with God, and to fan the spirit of Christianity in my own bosom, to have constant recourse to them.[1]

In perusing the writings of Oberlin, we see that he had fortified his soul against such backsliding against which Stouber had warned. He constantly dedicated himself to God afresh; he fed his spiritual life and bathed his soul in the Word of God and in prayer. As a man is impoverished or enriched physically according to his eating habits, so he is strengthened spiritually with might in the inner man by long meditations on the Bread of Life which gives permanence and perseverance to his labors for God. Oberlin's biographer makes the following comments on this aspect of his life:

Except in his younger years, he read little but his Bible. His conversation was never more eloquent, nor his views more expanded than when he talked on the subject of the extension of the kingdom of God. . . . He continually looked to God as his *Papa celeste,* present with him, and rested all his hopes in Jesus, the author and finisher of our faith.[2]

The Bible itself, "la chere Bible," as he exclaimed with tears of gratitude a short time before his last illness, was the grand source of all his instructions. It formed the study of his life, and, as he said, constituted his own consolation under all trials, the source of his strength, and the ruling principle of his actions: how then, could he do less than recommend it to others? He was in the habit of citing very largely from it, from the conviction that the simple exposition of the Word of God was the best means of efficaciously interesting his flock.[3]

Sixteen years after he began his ministry, this innovative shepherd, longing for his flock to be nurtured in the faith, established "The Christian Society." The rules of this society were summarized in his own handwriting and translated from the original. We quote some of these below:

    1. Regeneration.
    2. Sanctification.
    3. "We are all one in Christ Jesus."
    4. "Abide in Me."
    5. "Christ is all, and in all."
    6. "Bring forth much fruit."
    7. "Love not the world, neither the things that are in the world."
    8. Nourish the inner man by:
    (1) The Word of God
    (2) Continual prayer
    (3) The frequent use of the Holy Sacrament. . . .[4]

"Millions of times," Oberlin wrote, "have I besought God to enable me to surrender myself with entire and filial submission to His will, either to live or to die: and to bring me into such a state of resignation, as neither to wish, nor to say, nor to do, nor to undertake any thing, but what He, Who only is wise and good sees to be best."[5]

Another safeguard which doubtless did much to keep him from the dangers his faithful advisor Stouber had foreseen was "the total renunciation of any thing like merit of his own." This "formed a remarkable and striking feature in Oberlin's character; he regarded himself merely as the instrument whom it had pleased God to employ, and was frequently heard to say: 'I have little merit in the good that I have done; I have only that of obedience to the will of God. He has been graciously pleased to manifest His intentions to me, and has always given me the means of executing them.'"[6]

He constantly urged his parishioners to pray without ceasing and had an ability to look beyond the sufferings and trials that often beset the pathway of the most devoted follower of Jesus Christ. His ability to persevere in most difficult circumstances with little encouragement from the outside world sprang from his firm conviction "that every event of our lives is under the guidance and direction of a superintending Providence. . . . In proportion as he suffered under affliction, his mind seemed to open to the consolations of faith."

I can remember hearing my pastor say that if one is really born again the purse strings would be loosened. He was doubtless referring to the older type of purse or bag which closed tight at the top with a drawstring. This could certainly be said of Oberlin, whose philanthropy involved great personal sacrifice. A letter from his own hand will best describe his unusual method of giving:

> You ask me for some explanation respecting the different tithes which God has commanded us to pay. I will tell you how I manage. I endeavor to devote three tithes of all that I earn, of all that I receive, and of all my revenue, of whatever name or nature it may be, to His service, or to useful objects.
>
> For this purpose I keep three boxes; the first for the first tithe; the second for the second; and the third box for the third tithe.
>
> When I cannot pay ready money all at once, I mark how much I owe upon a bit of paper, which I put into the box; and when, on the contrary, a demand occurs which ought to be defrayed by one of the three allotments, and there is not sufficient money deposited, I advance the sum, and make the box my debtor, by marking upon it how much it owes me.
>
> By this means I am always able to assist in any public or charitable undertaking, and as God has Himself declared that "it is more blessed to give than to receive," I look upon this regular disbursement of part of my property rather in the light of a privilege than a burden.
>
> The first of the aforementioned boxes contains a deposit for the worship of God. . . . The second box contains tithes for useful purposes. . . . The third box contains tithes for the poor.[7]

It is evident from the above that a more meticulous man could scarcely be found. He would keep an account of all his expenditures and had a record of each person in his parish and their condition. In case he should forget anyone, he placed their names upon the door of his study. As might be expected, Oberlin owed no man anything. He did not believe in debts and advised his hearers to beware of them as they would evil and wicked spirits.

Hard times befell the community of Ban de la Roche during the French Revolution. Oberlin's salary was withdrawn, but he told his people he would still minister to them without such. He offered refuge to those exiles who had escaped the guillotine and sword. His benevolence was far beyond what most would have thought necessary and he urged others to follow his example. For instance, if someone in the parish lost a cow, his neighbors would be encouraged to help compensate for the loss. As Oberlin's biographer puts it:

> He used his utmost endeavors to persuade others to imitate his example, and to avoid any superfluity in their clothes or manner of living, that they might be the better able to assist their poorer neighbors. . . . "Various mothers are, I observe, beginning to put frills of muslin or of cambric to their children's shirts. Do not do so, dear friends. Unpick them, cut them off, and seek not to increase the vanity of your children, which is already naturally too great. Cut off all the finery that does not correspond with your station in life, and employ yourselves in clothing the poor families of this extensive parish, many of whom are in an extremely miserable condition."[8]

He encouraged his women who came to listen to his sermons to knit stockings, not for their own families, but for the poor and indigent of the neighborhood. Many might feel this was a strange indulgence to grant his listeners, but because some would complain of sleepiness, he felt that knitting would help to keep them awake and benefit others at the same time.

Having mentioned so many good traits in this man of God, it is necessary to be reminded that we "have this treasure in earthen vessels" that the glory might not redound to man but to his God. Some would doubtless have criticized Oberlin and even refused to believe he was God's messenger because of his use of snuff. It was clear, however, that he refused to allow this habit to gain control, and would put the snuff on another floor of the house so that it was not easily accessible.

In reading his biography, we find that he was also of a fiery nature:

> The great-granddaughter explained to a visitor that Oberlin had at least one fault. He was hot tempered, and sometimes, when moved with impatience, would run back and forward in his study, beating his hands together rapidly with a resounding noise. At other times he would send the children flying off on different errands, 'like a hail storm.' Sometimes he would enforce a strong expression by flinging his cap off his head. He was also fond of his own way and rather arbitrary in carrying out his plans.[9]

It must be remembered that often relatives of a man of God, failing to understand the spiritual excellencies of their own kith and kin, are the most ready to enlarge on their deficiencies. Even so, we have added this that no man might receive the glory that comes from God alone. That is why the earthen vessel often bears marks that show that he is but man that we might honor the God Who called him and strengthened him for fulfilling the plan of the Almighty.

Whatever may have been his failings, there is no question about Oberlin's singleness of heart and motive. Often when Christ met a soul in need, He would ask, "What wilt thou that I should do for you?" Often their answer would serve to show the person's veracity and singleness of desire. Oberlin expresses his heart's desire in the following words taken from a letter written to one of his scholars:

> But I have still one wish—a wish that though I am old in years is always fresh in my heart—a wish that reigns predominant in my thoughts and never forsakes me. It is that my parish might make one solemn feast before God, a general and universal dedication, and one in which all persons without distinction might partake, every one ac-

cording to his respective ability. That is, a dedication of the heart in honor and remembrance of, and faith in Him, Who shed His blood for us in Gethsemane, and permitted Himself to be smitten, scourged, and spit upon, crowned with thorns, and nailed to the cross, that we might receive the Heaven which our sins had forfeited. This is the dedication that I so much desire every soul in my parish might join together to make—even the surrender of himself to Jesus, each one as he is, with all his faults, with all his sins, in order to find in Him, pardon, righteousness, sanctification, and redemption.[10]

With such a pastor to care for the flock, it is no wonder that after only five years of labor, the population which had formerly consisted of eighty or one hundred families, had increased to five or six hundred, constituting altogether three thousand souls. Visitors to Ban de la Roche were greatly impressed by the fruitful and arduous labors of a shepherd who stayed in his isolated parish for sixty years. When Charles Finney and Asa Mahan founded a college in Ohio, they named it Oberlin in honor of the man who had undertaken such a stupendous task.

A Swiss gentleman of some means, Mr. Legrand, who had been impressed with the work done in Ban de la Roche, decided to settle there and establish a factory for weaving silk ribbons. He became the superintendent of the schools and a few words from him explain his devotion:

It is now four years since I removed here with my family; and the pleasure of residing in the midst of a people, whose manners are softened and whose minds are enlightened by the instructions which they receive from their earliest infancy, more than reconciles me to the privations which we must necessarily experience in a valley separated from the rest of the world by a range of surrounding mountains.[11]

Several English women who visited the area give us a further insight into the beneficial results of years of painstaking labor:

I never knew so well what the grace of courtesy was till I saw this remarkable man. He treats the poorest people and even the children with an affectionate respect. For instance, his courtesy, kindness, and hospitality to our postillion were quite amusing. He pulled off his hat when we met him, took him by the hand, and treated him with really tender consideration. He is, I think, more than eighty—one of the handsomest old men I ever remember to have seen—still vigorous in mind and spirit—delighting in his parish—full of fervent charity. . . .

He shakes hands with all the little children as he passes them in the street, speaking particularly to each of them. The effect which such treatment has had in polishing these people, uncivilized and uncultivated as they formerly were, is quite wonderful. They have been taught a variety of things which have enlarged and refined their minds; besides religion—music, geography, drawing, botany, etc. . . .

If you go into a cottage they quite expect you will eat and drink with them; a clean cloth is laid upon a table washed almost as white as milk, and the new milk and the wine, and the great loaf of bread are brought out. Yet they are in reality exceedingly poor. Their beds also look so clean and good that they would astonish our poor people. In some respects I think they are decidedly cleaner than our own peasantry. . . .

The poor charm me. I never met with any like them; so much spirituality, humility, and cultivation of mind, with manners that would do honor to a court; yet the homely dress and the simplicity of the peasant are not lost. . . . The young people have long been in the habit of receiving religious instruction from their pastor, so that a gradual and imperceptible improvement, resembling the growth of plants in a well-cultivated garden, has taken place.

You may form some estimate of their moral progress, by the spirit of charity which manifests itself on occasion of the death of a poor father or mother leaving a numerous family. And by the eagerness with which the relations, friends, or neighbors of the deceased, take charge of the children, not to treat them as strangers and dependents, but as members of their own household. . . . This delightful spirit of benevolence particularly manifests itself also, in the eager alacrity with which the young people assist the old and feeble in their rural labors. . . .

I will just mention as a single instance among many others, of the transforming power of religion, that one young woman refused to marry that she might devote her time, her talents, and her strength to works of benevolence. And, allowing herself only the bare necessaries of life, she presented the fruits of her assiduous and unremitting industry to the excellent and pious institutions of the present day. She also sold all that she thought she could do without, and gave the produce to such objects as she believed calculated to advance the kingdom of our adorable Lord and Savior.[12]

Perhaps it would be well to end this sketch with a further tribute to the man who was faithful to his call and to his God right to the end. The following letter was translated from the journal of a French gentleman after his visit to Ban de la Roche. He was so tremendously impressed with what he saw there, that he had the account published in a German magazine:

During the space of nearly thirty years, in which M. Oberlin has been Christian pastor of this canton, he has completely changed it. The language is from an unintelligible patois, altered into pure French. The manners of the people, without degenerating, are civilized and ignorance is banished without injuring the simplicity of their character. Many of the women belonging to his parishes, trained for the purpose under his paternal care and instruction (and called "conductrices"), assist him in his occupations. They teach reading, writing, and the elements of geography, in the different villages where they reside. Through their medium the children are instructed in many necessary things, but above all have the seeds of religion and morality sown in their hearts.

The excellence of these schools is so well established and appreciated, that girls of the middle ranks are sent to him from distant parts, and the title of a scholar of Pastor Oberlin is no less than a testimonial of piety, cleverness, and gentle manners. His countenance is open, affectionate, and friendly, and bears a strong impress of benevolence. His conversation is easy, flowing, and full of imagination, yet always adapted to the capacity of those to whom he is speaking.

In the evening we accompanied him a league on his way back to Waldbach. We had a wooded hill to ascend; the sun was just setting, and it was a beautiful evening. "What sweet thoughts and pious sentiments you have uttered, during this interesting walk," said M. Oberlin, in a tone of confidence; for he considered us as friends to religion, and servants of God. Our hearts were indeed in unison; and he related to us the circumstances of his past life, and spoke of his views and ideas, and the fear and love of God, in a most touching manner.

Samuel Pollard

"AMIABILITY" is what his brothers and sisters called Samuel, on account of his unbounded good nature and affability. When tests and trials followed one another in rapid succession during his later life as a missionary in China, Samuel Pollard was glad that nature had endowed him with this bright outlook.

He was also grateful for the marvelous heritage which was bequeathed to him through his godly parentage. The older we grow, and the more we study biography, the more we are convinced that great advantages belong to those children born of praying parents who have surrounded and nurtured their child even before birth with prayer and dedication. All through manhood, Samuel Pollard never lost that deep reverence and respect he had for those who had so deeply cared for him from his infancy.

His father, Samuel Pollard senior, labored for a time as a mechanic in the dockyards at Chatham, but was later called to the itinerant ministry with the Bible Christian Society. The invisible God was to him no abstract Being, but a living Person in Whose presence he spent hours, pouring out his heart for those about him who had no knowledge of so great salvation.

When he met Ellen Deboyne of French-Canadian extraction, he was fascinated by her vivacity and deeply religious outlook. She left her teaching post to marry Samuel when he was thirty-one years of age. Their third child was named after the father and yet three more children were added to the family after his birth. Three times a day the father held family worship with his growing family, reading the Bible and praying himself, after which the children each added their petitions.

The father's lively imagination and emotional nature blended with the mother's readiness of wit, clear-cut thinking, and practical ability, making a wonderful combination in the training of Samuel, who was to become a future pioneer. Another valuable asset was that their home could not boast of luxuries, for the budget had to be stretched again and again to meet the needs of a family of six children. "There was plenty of love, but little money," wrote a sister. When very young, Samuel heard the conversations of father and mother regarding the shortage of funds, and took a lively interest in trying to augment their meager income by running errands for the neighbors.

When Samuel was seven the family moved to Penryn, Cornwall, and he was sent to a Wesleyan day school. Four years later, a momentous event altered the child's outlook on life. Many years afterwards, when a missionary in China, he would look back gratefully to this time as the beginning of his awareness of God and His mercy.

As a child, he had sat in the pew listening to his father's preaching, sensing the awe and wonder which accompanied the preacher and which would settle down over the audience as the minister pictured Redemption through Christ Jesus. Young Samuel longed to experience this mighty salvation. One night, he and his brother Walter had gone upstairs to bed, and the father, mounting the steps as was his usual habit to give the final tuck-in and good-night kiss, found that Samuel was still on his knees. Knowing what was transpiring, the father retired from the room with a heart full of rejoicing. He went up a second time but came away again, and when a third time he entered the room, Samuel's heart had already found peace. He was now God's child, born anew into the family of God.

Small as the family budget was, the parents were willing to sacrifice even more to send their boy to a school for ministers' sons which had been founded by the Bible Christian Society. Before leaving home, he had promised his father not to fight when at school. He kept his promise faithfully, though some of his fellow-students could have endured his fist easier than the potency of his tongue-lashing. They were made to feel the stinging scorn in his rebukes when any school mate would indulge in nasty jokes about "family purity." But, though mischievous and full of fun, Samuel would unashamedly bring out his New Testament every night and thus filled his mind with its priceless store of wisdom. At this school he won first-class honors in local Oxford exams.

At seventeen, after passing seventh in his exams for civil service, he went to London to fill a position at the Post Office Savings Bank. How delighted he was to think that now, earning a wage, he could reimburse his family for their sacrifice.

Circumstances now favored Samuel in that, nearby, was a chapel belonging to the Clapham Bible Christian Society which he was able to attend. Rev. F. W. Bourne*, the minister, made a lasting impression on the youth. His "vigorous intellect" and "massive moral force" combined with the "inward life of a mystic" influenced Samuel during the years 1881 to 1887. Later, when facing fiery ordeals on the mission field, he was buoyed up by the remembrance of such a "spiritual giant" as Mr. Bourne, pouring out his heart's best to twenty young people in such an obscure chapel when he could have commanded much greater audiences elsewhere.

About this time, missionaries from the China Inland Mission were doing deputation work in London, and a number of Samuel's close Cornish friends had offered themselves as missionaries to China under the Bible Christian Society. In a letter which startled his mother he wrote, "Vanstone and Thorne have just left for China, and I shall be the next." His mother felt she could not let her boy go, and this troubled Samuel who was devoted to her, but in a remarkable way, what would have been his most difficult obstruction was removed in answer to prayer.

At a watch-night meeting at Clapham, Samuel arose and asked the prayer group to specially petition God to soften his mother's heart so that she would consent to his going abroad. In the mean-

---

* Author of *Billy Bray The Kings Son*

time, in another watch-night service at St. Just in Cornwall, the parents were kneeling in prayer, and the Spirit of God was strangely speaking to Mrs. Pollard. Finally, after a struggle, she said, "Lord, I am willing." Her son's prayer had been answered, and now the way was open for Samuel Pollard to offer himself for China.

Another friend, Frank John Dymond, the son of a minister of the same denomination as the Pollards, offered himself as well. These two were destined to be close friends for many years in China, with nothing to mar their fellowship in the Lord. Their natures were just opposites, but this made each contribute something to the other. Together they set sail from Tilbury Docks in 1887 for their destined field—China. And together the two enthusiasts stepped ashore on March 14, and lost no time in having their hair cut, and donning gowns in true Chinese fashion.

Soon they entered the China Inland Mission Training Center at Ganking where for six months they strove to become familiar with this most difficult of languages—Chinese. "The road to the heart of this language is long—very long," Samuel wrote, "but even the longest roads are pleasant when walking in company with the Master."

At the C.I.M., this studious candidate excelled in his studies as usual. Writing to his parents he announced, "This week our big exam has come and now it is gone, for which I am delightfully thankful. The results were published at dinner-time today. . . . Will you be glad to know that your boy's name headed the list? Thank God for all His mercies! Out of a possible 400, I obtained 392."[1]

Before completing his training, however, a desire for a deeper experience had been growing upon him. He wrote confidingly to his parents:

> For some time past we have all been praying, more or less for more power. As the time was drawing near for our being thrust out into the work, we began in earnest to cry for the anointing service. Almost unknown to each other we were nearly all doing this. One is

very apt when studying hard day after day to let study take the first place; this some of us had done with consequent loss of spiritual life.

On Saturday 23 July, after the others were in bed, I determined I would get a blessing before I got up from my knees, and, thank God, I did. Sunday 24th came, and the person who took our service in the evening seemed to speak for all of us, and afterwards we adjourned to the top of the house for a prayer-meeting. . . . What was the result? A mighty blessing like to shake the house. Some of us got very happy, and the scene which followed was just like some of our old Pensilva or Penryn revivals. I was about the noisiest! By simple faith we laid hold of the power held out to us. . . .

I shall never forget that moment. Bless God, the power came immediately, and today, after more than two weeks, I am a different fellow. . . . We appear to have alarmed the natives in the surrounding houses. They came on Monday morning to inquire who was dead in the house. With them a death always occasions a lot of shouting and crying. They were quite right: several of us died that night, and the life we now live, we live by faith in the Son of God.[2]

The time soon arrived when Dymond and he set out on that long journey to Yunnan.

The scenery is indescribably grand; up and down cliffs, and over rugged rocks, we ride and tramp all day. Once we had to go along a ledge where there was scarcely room to walk; passing a fine waterfall I stopped and looked; it almost took my breath away. Dare I take the pony across such a path? One false step and we should be hurled down an abyss. A few moments of nerve tension and of desperate resolve, and we were over in safety. On the other side of the river, the cliff rose in a sheer mass for a thousand feet. What an echo was here![3]

A short paragraph by his biographer shows how Pollard was beginning to know the value of those early morning hours before the business of the day should interfere with his coming to know God better. "Sometimes in that hour before dawn when the stars die out and the sun has not risen, Pollard would lie and pray passionately for this land and its people. But as full wakefulness came he would leap up, and . . . hastily prepare for another day's work."[4]

It was a Wednesday evening on February 8, 1888, when the two young men of twenty-four entered the city of Chaotong which was to become their home. The Thornes were already there, and Mr. Thorne wrote home about the two: "You speak of them as 'choice spirits;' they are indeed two splendid men for the work."

Already the Lord of harvests was training His new men through the long, tedious, day-by-day labors so necessary before many results could be realized. "In spite of our rough surroundings," Samuel wrote, "we young fellows got on all right, for our hearts were brave, and we were soldiers of the King and willing to endure for His sake." They were learning too that dependence upon God for every bit of help was of vital necessity. "We never started without prayer," said Dymond; "then, too, each prayed for the other as we preached." The curious, gaping crowds sometimes mounting to a thousand were at first hailed as a delight, but when the missionary, tired or spent, had to endure the curiosity of the multitude, it could be disconcerting.

But it was not only their strange surroundings which sometimes disconcerted the two new missionaries. They were also to know frustrating and inexplicable delays caused by illness. After one of their usual evangelistic efforts, each having gone in a different direction, Dymond came home with an aching head and weary body. There was no doctor within two months' journey of Chaotong. After searching through medical books, Sam decided that his friend had that dreaded disease—smallpox. He now took the place of doctor, nurse, cook, and housekeeper and for none of these was he trained. To make his task more difficult, there were few supplies of any food to suit such an invalid. It was small wonder that once, when delirium gave way to a sober moment, Dymond longed for death to relieve him.

This caused the usually happy Pollard some apprehensions, and when the sick man saw this, he suggested a communion service:

> A couple of Chinese cups, a small pot of tea, and a Chinese biscuit were all we needed. But the nurse broke down and the sick man

had to finish the service. I can assure you that Jesus Himself came to us in that little upper room, and we were wonderfully cheered and comforted by His love and presence. Death seemed to lose all its terrors, and instead there came a vision of glory, a vision of triumphant entrance into the King's presence.[5]

For four weeks Pollard never undressed, and there were nights when he did not know whether his patient would expire before morning. It was a slow rising up out of the valley and shadow of death, but what a joy when Dymond was well enough to climb down the ladder with Pollard below him in case he fell.

The new recruits were being trained by the Heavenly Lord of the Harvest. Gradually the truth was dawning upon them that it might take twenty years before the seed sown would yield a harvest, and it would require a still longer period before those new converts could be taught the terms of discipleship.

But the time had now come when these inseparable companions who had been together for over a year were to part company. The Society had felt it best for each to labor in different areas. They must have felt the parting deeply, but they were now mature enough to stand the loneliness which separation brings. Dymond went northward, while Pollard prepared himself for a ten days' mission in Yunnan Fu.

It was at this time that God gave an intimation to His servant what lay in the future. A letter written in 1888 will best describe the remarkable revelation given to Pollard at that time:

A week of prayer preceded the meetings, during which one day was spent in fasting. . . . Last Sunday week we had seven hours at the work. Glorious meetings, and I believe many were brought face to face with salvation as they had never been before. Several professed openly a desire to serve Jesus Christ, and the greatest friendliness has been shown us all through the meetings. Tuesday, the ninth day, was spent in fasting, and was followed by a night of prayer.

I shall never forget it. Our room was filled with glory, and I had a manifestation such as I had never realized before. The glory came down and so filled me that I felt the Holy Ghost from my head to the soles of my feet. It was about as much as I could stand, and for a minute I thought I should faint or die. . . . I had the promise at that meeting that we are going to have thousands of souls. Mind, I believe that from the bottom of my heart. . . . Some folks may say, "He's a fool!" Let them; we'll have our thousands. "He's gone mad." So be it; but we'll have our thousands. "He's young and enthusiastic." Yes, glory be to God, I am; and we'll have our thousands. . . .[6]

And Pollard did live to see that promise amply verified. Sixteen long years were to intervene before the answer came—years of soul-training when fleshly ardors had subsided and faith tested through long weary journeys with few visible results. Sunshine and shadow, joy and sorrow, disappointments and blessings, good report and evil report—all would mature the youthful, buoyant spirit. But we must fill in some of those intervening years before we bring Pollard into the place of fulfilled blessing.

When a soul yields himself completely to his Master, then He undertakes to give the grueling training necessary to make him His yielded servant. For example, God used an awkward mule to teach Pollard patience. He tells us in his own words: "Went out to tea-shop. . . . On the way my mule fell down and I was off, and he was on my leg. . . . I thought I must punish the beast, and then as it would not come on, I kicked it. Afterwards, I felt sorry: God saved my life and instead of being grateful I got into a temper. May the Lord purify me wholly, and make me His own and forgive my sin!"

Later God confronted His servant with the choice as to whether or not he would adapt his life more and more to the pattern laid down by Jesus, the great Forerunner. Many see no need to follow Christ as He walked through this world, but there have been noble souls who have felt it their privilege to "walk as He walked."

John Wesley, for example, strove to exemplify as much as possible the lowly Nazarene; his life was a model of frugality and generosity. He realized, however, that what finally ate out the vital life of Methodism was riches. His first converts were frugal; they had few vices such as smoking, drinking or worldly pleasure to drain their pocketbooks, and so riches increased. Sad to say, this increase, not being shared with others less fortunate but rather used for luxuries, was to eventually crowd out the Man of Nazareth from Methodism.

Just when Pollard needed someone with whom to share his new light, Frank Dymond again appeared on the scene after an absence of six months. He had been asked to escort a nurse, who was to join Mrs. Thorne, through territory new to her, thus bringing him into contact with Pollard once more. A diary reading shows how these two earnest young men both wished to advance in the life of Christ. "February 25th: Frank and I had much talk about coming down to the level of the people (i.e. in their mode of living). I believe we are right and that God is working upon our hearts. The Lord help us and give us strength to go forward on the right lines whatever they may be! Frank says resolutely he will do it; he will come down to the level of the coolies and others." They discussed the subject of adopting this life of poverty and self-denial with their senior missionary. "He will not do this himself," Pollard tells us, "but he will give me every help if I am called to such a mode of life. I wish I knew what to do; may the Lord guide me very plainly."

Then, just when he was so keen to get on with the work, Pollard had to learn that frequent interruptions can also be used to train the zealous missionary. Their colleague, Mr. Vanstone, took ill, and someone was required to help nurse him back to health. Frequent attacks of malaria had reduced his resistance, and for five weeks Pollard would have to conduct his regular services and then aid in the nursing of his patient. No sooner had Mr. Vanstone recovered, than his wife took ill. But the darkest night usually precedes the dawn. Death ever precedes life in the spiritual realm, and the worker who insists upon the life of the Holy Spirit must always be delivered unto death if the life of Jesus is to be made manifest.

These stressful times took their toll on Pollard's health. On his way back to Chaotong he visited the barber and awoke to find himself lying on the mud-floor trying to remember what he had been dreaming about. Perspiration poured from him. "I had fainted in the heart of China, and I had the cheek to say in Chinese: 'This is my thorn in the flesh.'" It was nature's red light to the hitherto robust missionary, warning him that he must not play with his limited supply of physical energy. For the rest of his life he was to be subject to such attacks. And he was learning that weakness is the requisite for spiritual strength.

It is not only the body, however, that must be taken care of. On the mission station one needs constantly to keep one's mind in trim or he may find mental deterioration imperceptibly setting in. Knowing this, Pollard read considerably. His Greek New Testament took priority. Among the other books he read were, Neander's *Life of Jesus*; Asa Mahan's *Out of Darkness into Light*, the Life of Paton, Wesley's Sermons, the Life of Mackay, Foster's Essays, and various novels and journals.

Although China was indeed a land of varying interests, life was not all novel and exciting for the young missionary. There was the inevitable cross that preaching Christ will always bring. Seldom could Pollard pass down the street without being sneered at as a "foreign devil." And grown men "spat to express their loathing and the women covered their noses to avoid the offensive smell of the stranger."

A Chinese scholar in later years paid this tribute to Pollard:

> He preached incessantly at the capital; and men laughed at him because they did not understand; but though reviled and persecuted, he was undaunted; for he knew it was the sowing time. Seeing that the people disbelieved, he strove to put forth still greater efforts; some teachers have come to us and then resenting the contumely paid to them, they have shaken the dust off their feet and retired. Not so did the teacher Pollard. Gradually, though the Chinese still withheld their belief in his message, they delighted to converse with him, for he never cherished any thought of his own superiority, but treated them as brothers."

Romance finally came to this lonely young man of twenty-six. Pollard often found fellowship at the China Inland Mission house. Among those devoted men and women he met was a Miss Hainge for whom he felt a special attraction, and Sam lost no time in contacting her by a note. Then came the anxious period while he waited for her answer. Writing home to his parents he shared these anxious moments with them.

> I calculated about the time she would be home and got down on my knees and prayed. Didn't I feel bad! What a morning I spent! After service I found a note addressed to me on my table. All right! Hallelujah! We had a long talk together in the evening at her house. When I returned I took her photo with me, and sat down and wrote another letter. Oh, Sam Pollard! Tell it not in Gath! Gone! Irretrievably gone!! But I am glad to be gone![7]

Most of God's servants have had their faith severely tested when considering marriage. God is anxious to give them good gifts, but their tried faith is more priceless to Him than the object quickly obtained. In the case of Sam Pollard, there was a waiting time when Miss Hainge felt she must first get the consent of her parents, and this could not be obtained in a hurry. It was seven months before letters containing their sanction could reach them.

After their marriage, they were to be further tested by separations for the sake of God's Kingdom, and when their family increased to four boys, his wife found it necessary, because of their education, to be absent from her loved partner for longer periods.

Meanwhile, the never-ending demands upon the time of the few on behalf of so many—giving out medicines, preaching, visiting and being visited, living in unhealthy surroundings, traveling under inclement weather conditions—all had taken their inevitable toll. Vanstone had repeated bouts of malaria which weakened him. "Death stalked with slow, unhesitant steps." Thorne had also become a prey to malaria which eventually took his life. Dymond felt under such stress that it seemed he would have to return to England. It was now that the little group owed much to the naturally buoyant spirit of Pollard during these very trying times. "A spirit of hilarity oppressed me," he said. "I often wish I was of a graver and more dignified habit. It is so rarely that I am really sober." "Amiability" was performing perfectly.

At last, after seven years of wearisome toiling, Pollard was able to baptize his first two converts. He had not forgotten the prayer-meeting when thousands were promised him, and his quiet, seemingly unconscious influence was preparing the way for the Lord's time of refreshing.

About this time, Pollard became deeply exercised about the aboriginal tribes to the north-east of Yunnan, though it was to be twelve years before he was to receive a call from scouts from these tribes, called the Miao, asking him to visit them.

> They are fine men, though they have no written language and no books. As they cannot speak Chinese we cannot reach them through this tongue. Mr. Vanstone has for a long time held that God intended me to do a work among them. I have thought of it, and if ever Jesus says, "Go," I will go straight off. . . .
>
> No missionary has ever yet visited these people; the mists never lift from their minds. The river Yangtsze is the boundary between their territory and the Chinese. They are fierce mountain clans living under their own chieftains almost independent of the Chinese. . . . They come down from their fastnesses in robber bands and "lift" the cattle and crops of the Chinese, and steal people for slaves. . . . I would like to go over and spend a month among these people.

A prayer during the New Year season of 1894 will reveal the heartfelt burden this man of God possessed:

> Let me live this year with one aim to glorify God: to preach for His glory: to live for His glory: to read and write for His glory. Oh, that the presence of God may always be with me, making me think of Him; not counting a day well spent but what is spent for Him only; not counting a sermon worth preaching unless it be preached only for God.[8]

Furlough at last came to the tired missionaries, and Pollard endeavored to picture the vast need to many people in the homeland. He objected violently to the term "foreign" missionaries:

> Why do you put the stigma of "foreign" on me? Is it because I go to some place that is not "home" to you? It is "home" to me. It is "home" to Jesus. There is no spot on earth which can be called "foreign" to Him; it is all His—part of His personal inheritance. He has made the world His home. If you call us "foreign" missionaries, you place us on a different footing from your home ministers.
>
> Then we are called "foreigners" in the lands where we carry on our work. "Foreigners" everywhere! Outcasts! Undesirable aliens! We share the reproach of Jesus. Nevertheless we are His home-missionaries; for it is His land we go to: we are saving His children, enjoying His love. There is nothing "foreign" in the whole wide world to Him— except sin.[9]

"We expect difficulties," he said on another occasion. "We shall be disappointed if we do not get them; but difficulties only show us the size of Christ's love." He no longer retained those youthful anticipations of immediate success. The dangers, deaths oft, illnesses, and routine plodding with little or no results had matured this ambassador of Christ.

It was at this time that the Committee made him Superintendent of the Mission, but he felt keenly the apathy of the home church regarding ample funds and personnel. However, help was to come from a different front. Stephen Lee, a Chinese student, came to the missionary for help and proved, in time, to be an invaluable helper. Indeed, they were to become as inseparable as were Jonathan and David. Speaking of his friend, Pollard wrote:

> A few months ago, a student belonging to a family in good circumstances came to us in distress about his sins. It is so unusual to find a Chinaman willing even to confess he has any sin, that the young man's case caused us great interest and joy. The struggle he had was a long one, and many were his ups and downs. At length he got the light wished for. . . and now he gives evidence of his communion with Jesus.[10]

For his part, Stephen Lee esteemed his new spiritual father highly:

> Seeing Mr. Pollard's deeds and hearing his speech, I judged that we had in China one who was unique. As I learned to know him I greatly admired the spirit that was in him: it was almost like seeing one of our sages reincarnated. After leading my elder brother into the church, we discussed with Mr. Pollard the whole question of education, and the result was that the Mission school was transformed. It became the fountainhead of Western learning in the province of Yunnan. . . . The Western teacher looked upon my brother and me as his hands and feet. We loved each other with virtue and courtesy.[11]

The first signs of the promised revival came on July 12, 1904, when four scouts from the Miao tribe came to Chaotong to inquire of Pollard and stayed from Tuesday until Saturday morning. They brought a letter from a missionary who felt he could not cope with the demands among the Miao, and so had sent those scouts to Pollard with a letter of introduction from himself.

How thrilled the missionary must have been, as those men told of an entire tribe waiting to hear the Gospel. Numbers began to visit him, until they increased to one hundred within little more than a month.

> They swarmed around us everywhere. Directly a door was opened, in they trooped with their books, begging to be taught. They began at five o'clock in the morning, and at one o'clock the next morning some of them were still reading. Cramming Christianity! Let a schoolboy but show his nose anywhere and a score of Miao would pounce upon him. . . . I can assure you it was a glorious but most disconcerting experience.[12]

These Miao needed little by way of hospitality as they traveled light. They brought their own oats which they would mix with water, and at night they laid down on the floor to sleep. The language barrier was the biggest problem, for Pollard did not know the Miao language, and there were so few among them who could speak Chinese. "We found but one man in two hundred who could read. . . . Our services were some of the most delightful I have ever seen. . . . How were we to begin?"

These ignorant hill people were very suspicious, having been the dupes of their witch doctors and wizards for centuries. They believed that Pollard possessed unusual powers. If he would but drop water on their tongues, they were enabled to speak. If he smoothed down the hair on the head, their memory suddenly took on supernatural ability to remember. But it was also rumored that he was giving these Miaos potions which, if given to their landlords, would poison them.

After their harvest was over, they trooped to Chaotong, filling up the mission houses. These ignorant men had never held a book in their hand before. Now they clutched at their flimsy books and applied themselves in earnest to learn the most difficult of languages. The danger now was for the health of Mr. Pollard. His wife grew anxious and one day persuaded her husband to go up to his bedroom, lock the door, and pocket the key. What was her surprise later to find him surrounded with a dozen of these men all eager and intent with their books and considering themselves highly privileged to have the missionary all to themselves. They had climbed the balcony, and looked into each room until they had discovered him.

Pollard and Stephen Lee now gave themselves up to the study of the Miao language. Within a few weeks, they were enabled to convey a simple message, and before long they were writing Bible stories for the natives in the easiest Chinese characters they could use. But how could they possibly explain to these people such ideas as sin, and prayer, and redemption?

Such an influx of visitors brought a few problems to the missionaries established at Chaotong, disturbing their usual routine. Some saw in this movement the possibility of great things; others viewed it as an interference with the work which had been started years before.

Then there was persecution as the overlords, who, noticing the moral change which was evident in the lives of their serfs, worried that they would become less amenable to oversight. Consequently, the new converts suffered loss of personal belongings; others were beaten and chained. But subservient as these serfs had formerly been to their masters, they now showed an obstinacy of purpose to remain true to their new-found, heavenly Master. To those held down by landlords for years, the thought of belonging to the great family of God was wonderful. That Jesus was their Elder Brother seemed too good to be true. That the Holy Spirit could inspire their minds and instruct their hearts was equally delightful news.

"The greatness of the work frightens one at times. What are we to do with it?" queried the tired missionary. "What does God mean us to do? If He says take up this work swiftly, then I shall have to obey." Pollard had by now taken to visiting their villages. Two hundred Miao came to the village to meet him, and they told him that within a radius of a few miles he could reach a thousand Miao families. In village after village he was received as a veritable angel of God. How different from the treatment accorded to Dymond and himself when they had first set foot in China.

Pollard may not have been strong, but in courage he was a giant, often bearding the lords in their castles on behalf of the persecuted minorities. "Despised and persecuted by their conquerors, the Chinese, the only love they have known is begotten of the Gospel! Beaten, chained, robbed, tortured, still they come, sometimes wearing Chinese dress as a disguise."

As this mass movement did not abate, the Conference decided that Pollard should be set aside for this work and relieved of his responsibilities at Chaotong. This placed a heavier burden on the already overtaxed missionaries, and caused some misunderstandings which the years did not clear away. But revival cannot come without its price to both those wrought upon and the instrument used in bringing it to pass.

Pollard had usually been most successful in quelling any serious trouble which might arise. In fact, it seemed he had divine assistance in his interviews with unsympathetic persons in authority. "Although thwarted for a time," his biographer tells us, "there were Chinese and No-Su lords who 'nursed their wrath to keep it warm.' Attempts upon his life had thus far failed, but he had presentiments that he would yet share in the sufferings of his Miao converts, though with the buoyancy of inveterate optimism, he shut these forebodings out of his mind." For three years now he had lived with that sense of danger. He could not afford to lessen his endeavors because of threats!

On a Monday morning, April 8th, he set out for Ha-lee-mee, arriving at five o'clock and receiving his usual welcome from the Miao. In the evening between eight and nine while he was teaching, there was a sound of rifle fire, but his host assured him that it was only the neighboring villagers firing shots to scare off the evil spirits. His host, however, was deceiving him, for soon the house was surrounded by men with weapons, shouting, "Kill" and "Murder." Not having time to escape as the door of his room was already being pushed open and his assailants were upon him, he went out to meet them. Sixty armed men surrounded him, and began to beat his Miao Christians.

When they reached the river, Pollard, thinking to make his escape, jumped down the bank and ran down the river bed, only to be overtaken. Here they beat him unmercifully, and he would perhaps have been killed, had not a tall Chinese who had always showed kindness to the Miao intercepted his assailants and threw himself on the prostrate missionary. In a letter to his wife Pollard later wrote: "Just as I expected eternity to dawn, a man with a sheepskin jacket stooped down, put his arms around me, and ordered the beating to cease."

The missionary was then taken to a walnut tree and, at first, it looked as if he would be hanged; then it was decided to conduct a trial in which he was accused of deceiving the people. Pollard tells us: "I had tried my legs before, now I tried my tongue and pleaded for all I was worth." The verdict was finally given; Pollard was told to leave the district and never return, and if he did return he would be killed. And it was made clear that if any action were taken against them for that evening's work, all the Miao in the village would be killed.

Later, when describing that terrible evening to his mother, he wrote:

> When lying in the hut unable to turn over, an old Miao came in—he is over six feet high and one of our best Christians—he smoothed down my hair gently and I could feel his tears falling on my bed. Then with a full heart he said: "Teacher, you must not die: you are like a father to us all. You tell us what to do and we do it. If you are gone who will direct and teach us? You must not die, teacher! Let me die instead of you!" So said the old man; a few years ago he was a drunkard and a terror in his home and to all his people.

Grace had won high degrees among these Miao but at a cost!!! Dr. Savin, who undertook to bring Pollard to the hospital at Chaotong, explained the extent of his injuries:

> On making a superficial examination I found that his body was a mass of bruises, the only part that had escaped injury being the head. On more closely examining him, I found that he had received a wound in one lung and that air had escaped into the surrounding tissues: one or more ribs were injured, or broken. The wound of the lung was just below the heart. For some days Mr. Pollard was in danger, as some pneumonia followed the lung injury. Mr. Pollard had a narrow escape of his life. If the blow that injured the lung had been delivered an inch higher he would have been killed on the spot. . . . At the time of writing, three weeks after the assault, Mr. Pollard is able to sit up in bed, but cannot turn on his right side. He still has considerable pain at the site of the injured lung. It will be some time yet before he will be able to leave his room, or will have recovered from the shock to his nervous system.

Mr. Pollard's recovery was slow. No one can attack the kingdom of darkness without being assailed by the Prince of this world. The price this missionary had to pay was that he never did overcome the blow his nervous system had received from so violent an attack. However, the work among the Miaos once again soon absorbed the interests of this modern St. Paul. As he viewed the immense possibilities of the field and the huge population devoid of doctors, teachers, and missionaries, his indignation would at times flare up against the slowness with which his friends and supporters at home met the challenge of this tremendous opening.

Consolidating the work was now the task of the worn-out missionary who still endured hardships in order to meet the demand upon his limited physical resources. Churches were built; schools were organized; medical attention was given to the sick; visitation of the various villages was dutifully carried out.

Once again he was advised to go home on furlough so as to regain his strength. While doing deputation work, he appealed to the people to come up to the help of the Lord and volunteer lives and money to respond to the call of a people so needy, not because of the idol worship or because of the "shames and miseries of Chinese childhood." No, he had learned something of the fellowship of His Savior's sufferings, and His words burned into his listeners as he asked them to go because "years and years ago a Friend of his was cruelly treated and betrayed. The literati of His day openly scorned Him and sought, by foulest means, His undoing and His death. They stirred up the people against Him, they circulated slanders, and then, with the help of the mob they had maddened, they dragged Him through the gate of the city and nailed Him to a tree." It was for His sake that the missionary asked his young hearers to go. "One thousand millions such as you and I—one Savior such as He—GO!"

Mr. Pollard was to experience a disappointment upon his return to the field, when he learned of the adverse decision of the District Meeting to divide up the field of labor among the Miao tribes. "I kept my counsel," he said in a letter, "said a word now and again. If I had attempted to fight it, or to dispute certain points there would have been fireworks. As it was I let them humiliate me. It was for the time a bitter dose, and I was absolutely alone. . . ."

But the worn soldier of the cross was to prove once again that "all things work together for good." The decision worked for the benefit of all concerned, for the lessened field of labor gave more time for Mr. Pollard to give to the translation of the New Testament into Miao. It was the Scriptures in their own language which was to be of inestimable value to these primitive, formerly illiterate peoples.

Looking back over the years spent on the field, Pollard commented, "Twenty-five years ago Frank and I left England for China. What mercies God has given us in this quarter of a century! How little I have really done for Him Who has done so much for me! It was worth coming. I would do it again if I had to go over it once more. The end of twenty-five years finds us out in China."

In viewing the medical difficulties of the Mission he wrote: "There are seven million souls in the province of Kweichow and no doctor! In Yunnan, where the population is estimated at twelve millions, there are three medical missionaries, though since Dr. Savin is on furlough we actually have only a lady, Dr. Lilian Grandin, for the extensive medical work in and around Chaotong." In fifty-one days he had dispensed: "340 doses of quinine; 580 doses of santonine—worm medicine; 490 packets for diarrhea; 130 doses of medicine for indigestion; seventy doses for headache. Total—1,610. These were all sent to out-stations."

It was wisdom and heavenly foresight that caused Mr. Pollard to train native helpers, for he was not to have a long life on account of the hardships he had endured as a pioneer of new territory. At fifty-one, this able missionary was called home. An epidemic of typhoid broke out in the school, and, despite all precautions, soon spread among the missionaries. Mr. Pollard's body, already weakened, could not resist the deadly disease. On September 15, 1915, his spirit winged its flight back to the God Who had called, sustained, protected, and used him extensively in revival effort among a people previously untouched.

His beloved Miao felt they owed their very souls to this spiritual father and begged to be allowed to oversee his funeral arrangements. "He is ours," they said. "Let us bury him; we will arrange for coffin, bearers, grave, and tombstone; for we loved him more than our fathers, and he was ever kind to us."

His old colleague, Frank Dymond, conducted the services at the graveside amidst the singing, prayers, and testimonies of a transformed people. What a tragedy it would have been if a certain gifted, Cornish youth had not, those many years before, left the allurements of home, career, comfort, and ease in order to "follow the Lamb whithersoever he went!"

George   Matheson
1842-1906

George Matheson

"He that descended is the same also that ascended up far above all heavens, that he might fill all things" (Eph. 4:10).

I WAS very proud in my small days," wrote George Matheson in one of his many books. "Ere yet I had been enlarged by Thee, I had no shrinking in my nature. I pitied the past, and proposed to set it right. I pitied the present, and purposed to excel it. But when I was put forth, brought out, given a post in advance, then it was that I felt humble. The flower of my life turned to the sun when it began to blossom; in its ripeness it looked to Thee. The proof of its summer was its sense of impotence, of inability to stand alone.

"Never let me lose this sense of impotence, this evidence of the kindled flower. Never let me lose that want of Thee which is the pledge that I am nearing Thee. I am only inspired when I have aspired—sighed for something above me. When I first saw Thee, I thought it was a light thing to reach Thee; I said, 'Bid me that I come to Thee on the waters.' But now the stream has become a river and the river has widened into a sea, and Thou art far before."[1]

The above was written when George Matheson was fifty-three, just eleven years before his death. He was "seeing" that in the spiritual realm, descent must precede ascent. The law that governs the material world is ascension. The god of this world hides from his devotee the inevitable descent which must eventually come. "Pride goeth before destruction and a haughty spirit before a fall," the Good Book predicts. Adam in the garden listened to the serpent, "Be as the gods," but theologians term this seeming ascent—"The Fall." This ambition to ascend marks every child born into this world; it even absorbs the man who fills the pulpit until he has seen God's view of this fateful injection of hell.

Because man ascended, the Son of Man must needs descend. In Ephesians 4:9-10 Paul speaks of this marked reversal in the order of things in the life of Christ. "Now that he ascended, what is it, but that he also descended **first** into the lower parts of the earth. He that descended is the same also that ascended up far above all heavens, that he might fill all things." "He that humbleth himself shall be exalted," spake the King concerning the principles governing His kingdom. "He who would reign must suffer," Paul reminded the young church.

A short meditation from the pen of Matheson reveals his grasp of this fundament law of the Kingdom of God. Commenting on 2 Cor. 4:10, he says:

> "Always bearing about in the body the dying of the Lord Jesus, that the life also of Jesus might be made manifest in our body." What an unhealthy state of mind, you say—to be ever fondling the idea of death! How can it manifest life to bear death in my body? Will it not sap my energy? Will it not make me a dreamer? Will I not lose all interest in the present world if I am always thinking of passing from earth to Heaven? Yes; but this is no common death of which the apostle speaks; it is the dying of the Lord Jesus.
>
> The dying of the Lord Jesus was not the passing from earth to Heaven; it was the passing from Heaven to earth. *Every step of His dying was a step downwards.* He took the servant's form. He took the human likeness. He took the fleeting fashion of a man. He took the image of the humblest man. He went down deeper than humility. He lost His personality in love. He became one with the poor, the outcast, the erring. He felt the pains that dwelt in other bodies, the griefs that lived in other souls, the sins that slept in other hearts.

At last He touched the lowest ground, and therefore the common ground—He completed His dying in the Cross. It was the final stage of His union with man. It brought Him into the heart of the world. It made Him in the deepest sense a citizen of time.

Say not, then, oh my soul, that to bear Christ's dying within thee is to lose thy hold of earth; it is to double that hold. It is to come from high thought into menial action. It is to empty thyself into the commonplace. It is to descend into what men call reality. It is to leave the green fields of speculation for the thorny paths of practice. It is to give up thy poetry for other people's prose, to resign thy sunlight for thy weak brother's candle. Art thou prepared for this sacrifice, oh my soul?[2]

If we were to follow the life of this great Christian thinker, we would mark the gradual stepping downward. It was just at the blush of life when George was but eighteen months old, that his mother was told that her promising young son had an inflammation of the eye that would eventually result in blindness. Matheson thus started life maimed. However, it was not until he was eighteen years old and a brilliant university student that darkness finally settled down upon him, robbing him of his precious sight.

A spark of spiritual life had been kindled in his heart while sitting under the preaching of William Pulsford in Glasgow. "The man of all others," he said, "that shaped my personality, was Pulsford. I met him only once, but I never heard a man who so inspired me; he set me on fire, and under God he was my spiritual creator."

In his beautiful and inspiring poem we can read his testimony to the entire submission of his whole being to Christ:

> Oh, how weary were the years
> Ere Thy form to me was known!
> Oh, how gloomy were the fears
> When I seemed to be alone!
> I despaired the storm to brave
> Till Thy footprints touched the wave.

But Thy presence on the deep
   Calmed the pulses of the sea,
And the waters sank to sleep
   In the rest of seeing Thee,
And my once rebellious will
Heard the mandate, "Peace be still!"
Now Thy will and mine are one,
   Heart in heart, and hand in hand,
All the clouds have touched the sun,
   All the ships have reached the land;
For Thy love has said to me,
"No more night!" and "No more sea!"

Jesus, Fountain of my days,
   Well-spring of my heart's delight,
Brightness of my morning rays,
   Solace of my hours of night!
When I see Thee, I arise
To the hope of cloudless skies.

It was not long before the blind preacher faced another descent while in the second year of his first ministerial appointment in the town of Innellan, Scotland. He was to go through an experience which shook the very foundations of his faith. Matheson lived at a time when new theological ideas were abroad and many were questioning their traditional training. He had come through university seemingly unscathed by the "speculative methods of the German philosophers" unlike many of his contemporaries. As his biographer puts it:

He was evidently content for the time being to walk in the old paths, and to light them up with flashes of imagination and poetry. He could not, however, live long in a frail house of this kind; the crash was bound to come, and when it did come his theological tabernacle was a mass of ruins. . . .

The result was a temporary unhinging, a threatened collapse of his religious beliefs. Nor should anyone express surprise at this, any more than he should at the break-down in the manner of his preaching. Both were bound to come. One cannot conceive a man like Matheson passing through life without being called upon to reconsider his theological bearings. He was brought up on the traditional beliefs of his day. His boyhood and youth were passed in a period of extreme orthodoxy.[3]

Many of us can testify to the awesome sense of insecurity which results from an acknowledgment that the traditions which we have held so dearly are in conflict with Biblical truth. The shallow waters of our beliefs must be exchanged for the ocean depths of God's eternal realities.

Years later Dr. Matheson refers to this soul-shaking experience: "At one time, with a great thrill of horror, I found myself an absolute atheist. After being ordained at Innellan, I believed nothing; neither God nor immortality. I tendered my resignation to the Presbytery, but to their honor, they would not accept it, even though a highland Presbytery. They said I was a young man, and would change. I have changed."[4]

As he began a most thorough and diligent study, he could see that a great deal of his theological upbringing had been merely according to tradition. As he searched to discover his fundamental beliefs he, to his amazement, discovered "the search to be in vain." As we read in his biography:

> He had in reality no fundamental beliefs to examine. He had accepted the traditional views, and had never really inquired into their absolute truth or their living relation to his own soul. Most men are content to pass on through life without ever questioning the doctrines which they inherit. They may be reputed to be orthodox, and are among the first to cast stones at those who dare to inquire. Matheson could not possibly be numbered with this class. The day of his visitation was sure to come; and it came to him like a thief in the night.[5]

His friends knew that it was "impossible for a spiritually-minded man like Matheson to remain for any length of time an atheist. The darkness could only be temporary; new light was sure to dawn upon the troubled mind." And they were right. Light did come and, throughout the coming years, he "stood fast in his profound belief in Christianity, in the ideas which it embodies. These he was convinced were from all time and for all time."

Dr. Matheson had been willing to forego that sense of assured poise which "being in the swim of the theological thought of the day" is bound to bring. God's truth is like an unfathomed deep, and when we leave the shore of man's circumscribed thinking, our theological feet cannot touch bottom.

A further prop was soon to be removed. Matheson was considered an able speaker, and he painstakingly wrote out his sermons. His blindness necessitated him memorizing his sermon as well as his hymns and Bible readings. His grasp of truth in his sermons attracted the summer tourists who thronged the small coastal town of Innellan during the summer months. One day, while standing in the pulpit, his mind became a blank. He asked the congregation to sing a song while he sat down to compose his thoughts. When he arose, he spoke on a Scripture which had been given to him in that very hour. This marked an important era in the life of the young preacher. His biographer comments:

> This must have happened in the year 1878, for I find that from that time onward none of his sermons are written out in full. Up to that period, sixteen volumes are filled with his discourses. . . . But from this time onwards there is a marked curtailment; the space in manuscript is reduced to a half, and, in a very short time, to a tenth part of what the sermon formerly occupied. He now adopted the method of preparing a skeleton only. Each skeleton seldom occupies more than a page, if so much.[6]

Sympathetic friends thought the task of memorizing hymns, Scripture lesson, and sermon might impose too great a burden on their beloved minister, and suggested that he allow his assistant to conduct the former part of the service.

Matheson objected strongly, saying, "Prayer never causes me an effort. When I pray I know I am addressing the Deity, but, when I preach, the devil may be among the congregation."

A minister, Rev. T. R. Varnett, while a student in Edinburgh, sought out a church where he could find bread for his soul. St. Bernard's Church, where Dr. Matheson was pastor for thirteen years, proved to be the final answer to his quest. This is his impression of his minister's prayers:

> Dr. Matheson's first prayer was often the finest part of the service. And what a prayer it was! A lifting up of the heart and upraising of the spirit, a reaching out after God, an outpouring of the soul, like the rapturous song of the lark, mounting higher and higher into the blue, to find in the limitless skies the satisfaction of its whole nature. I confess that it was the first prayer that often lifted us up into the Mystic Presence more than any other part of the service.
>
> How difficult it was to keep the eyes closed! There upon the high pulpit was the blind poet, with uplifted hand, always reaching out and up into his own illumined darkness, as if trying to catch something of the mystery of God and draw it down to man. He carried us all up into the heights, along with him; and he drew down, for the most commonplace of us, something of the transfiguring blessing; so that often before the rapture of aspiration was over, the eyes that watched the blind, praying man in the pulpit had to view him through a mist of unconscious tears. How many of our preachers draw tears from the eyes of the worshipers as they pray? Through the man's aspirations, God laid His hand on the heart of us all.

How this godly preacher and writer was led into a life of communion with God, we are not told, but prayer became an integral part of his life. No man who is prayerless is a humble man sensing his utter helplessness. A prayerless man is a confident man, if he dares to stand before his people without first bowing in the awesome presence of Deity for some time so that he might give his listeners a "thus saith the Lord."

Matheson evaluates prayer in one of his meditations: "Prayer is no lesson for the beginner; it is for the last year. It is thy mark for the highest prize. Before it can be reached by thee, thou must love all beautiful things—the hallowed name, the coming Kingdom, the accepted will, the brother's bread, the forgiven debt, the redeemed evil."[7]

D. Macmillan, in his biography of Dr. Matheson's life, says: "Most of his life, indeed, was spent in close fellowship with the Father of Spirits. His hours of solitude were seasons of communion. He never felt himself to be alone, and though he could not see the outward world he peopled a world of his own with the spirits of just men made perfect."

In his book, *Searchings in the Silence*, each of the short meditations ends with a prayer, which in many cases occupies half the reading. In several of his other books he concludes each chapter with a prayer. Speaking to the Father was so easy a transition from speaking to his people, that he would direct his prayers to God in the midst of his sermonizing. These addresses to God are striking in their variety and spontaneity.

> In place of bringing the truth home to his hearers, as is the practice of most preachers, he brought his hearers home to the truth; carried them up into a region of Divine communion, and lifted their souls above the things of time and of sense to those which are unseen and eternal. . . . He had found how unsatisfactory all purely formal teaching is. He had fought his way to the surface, and he held the truth as he had found it through spiritual storm and stress, with a tenacity which no power could break, and he presented it with an intellectual conviction, and under an imaginative glow which carried his hearers captive.[8]

The descent of Dr. Matheson is perhaps most clearly traced in his books. He began with highly theological thoughts and philosophical discoveries. At thirty-two, he was writing *Aids to the Study of German Theology;* three years later he published, *The Growth of the Spirit of Christianity* in two volumes which found little sale. At forty years of age he began to publish his meditative works, short readings on selected Bible verses, each ending with a prayer. In these, one senses that he has been illuminated by the same Spirit which inspired the original writers of Scripture. The test of a good book, someone has said, is that it enlightens as one reads. These readings most certainly do. One is inspired with the freshness of thought and the enlarged understanding of the Scriptures.

George Matheson also penned wonderfully inspiring hymns such as "O Love That Will Not Let Me Go" and "Make Me a Captive Lord," and we have told how the former brought much blessing to broken hearts in our book *Handicaps, Volume Two*.

From age forty-eight to fifty, Dr. Matheson studied deeply into the life of St. Paul, and gave to the public a marvelous development of this inspired writer in his three requests for the removal of the thorn. He so aptly shows how St. Paul's advance and descent into deeper life of Christ had its effect upon his writing of the epistles. This book was considered by many as George Matheson's best and sold very rapidly.

"His earliest books and articles," writes D. Macmillan, "deal with subjects which are purely theological and philosophical. They are themes that are, so to speak, in the air; they interest the mind of man, and at first sight they do not seem to have much relation to or influence on his life. But as the years advanced, new subjects present themselves. They are in a sense more real, more human, more personal."

His last work was *Studies of the Portrait of Christ* in two volumes, written just six years before his death. He had found the central figure in history—Jesus Christ Himself.

> The life and teaching of the Savior became to him the one theme worthy to be dealt with and the volumes that he wrote on this and kindred topics were the most popular and influential ever published by him. His progress like that of the apostle was a de-

scent. He began with subjects of lofty thought; he contented him-self at the end with lowly themes, but these themes after all were the only vital ones for they were common to the heart of humanity and came into contact with man's experience at every point.[9]

The worship of Christ, which the young convert is asked to regard as the first step in the new life was, in a sense, the last in the career of Dr. Matheson. I do not desire to be misunderstood. That worship pervaded his life, but it was only towards its close that it ripened into full maturity and took possession of his whole nature. If in his early years, his ambition was to find in Christianity a solution of the problems which vex human reason, in his later years it was his absorbing desire to find in Christ Himself the solace of the human heart and the satisfaction of the human spirit. His own development, like that of his Master, was also in its nature a descent. It witnessed the fall of his spirit from the heights of theology to the prosaic plains of religion; from the effort to cleave the skies on the wings of thought to the patient sitting at the feet of the Master. It was there at last that he found peace.[10]

The sense of absolute dependence is the real basis of religious belief. To feel our limitation is the first step towards a conception of the infinite. "Faith," he remarks, "is essentially a Christian term. It differs from religious belief in general, as the species differs from the genus. Belief is the recognition of a Divine principle, faith is the recognition of a Divine principle which bears to us a moral relation . . . the sense of absolute dependence."

Several prayers contained in his meditations reveal to us how completely this servant of the Lord had learned the lesson of descending that he might ascend to the heavenlies and there be seated with Christ.

But now Thou appearest in mean attire. The purple and fine linen are exchanged for sackcloth and ashes. The crown has been cast into the sea, the glory has been buried in the dust, and, in its room, Thou carriest a cross of great pain. My old nature shrinks back from Thee; Thou art no more the spirit of its dream. But, as it sleeps, my heart waketh. My new life rises on the ruins of the old. My love becomes rich as Thou becomest poor; I find my star in

Thy night. I come to Thee in the gate of Golgotha; I meet Thee in the place of tears; I join Thee in the valley of humiliation; I descend with Thee to the spirits in prison.

Where Thou goest I shall go. Death itself shall not separate between Thee and me. Death with Thee were worth eternity without Thee; pain with Thee were worth joy without Thee; hell with Thee were worth Heaven without Thee.

Thou art the only pearl in my sea; Thou art the only gem in my sky; Thou art the only song in my soul. Pilate may divest Thee of Thy robes, but he cannot rob Thee of Thy beauty. My love can see Thy kinghood in Thy cross; Thy poverty has made me rich.

O Thou Divine Spirit, I bless Thee that by Thy poverty Thou hast enriched my love. Often in the days of old hast Thou come to me with the purple and the fine linen, and the sumptuous faring; and I was glad to be with Thee, not because Thou wert beautiful, but because Thou wert profitable. I arose and followed Thee because I left nothing.[11]

Lord, give the blessing of Jacob—his best blessing—his power to bless. . . . Make it impossible for me to stay at the top of the ladder, even though that be Heaven. Send me down the golden stair, down to the pillows of stone, down to the limbs which are languid, down to the souls which are sad! Send me with a breath of Eden, send me with a flower of Paradise, send me with a cluster of the grapes of Canaan! Send me to the hours which precede the daybreak, those darkest hours which come before the dawn!

Send me to the hearts without a home, to the lives without a love, to the crowds without a compass, to the ranks without a refuge! Send me to the children whom none has blessed, to the famished whom none has fed, to the sick whom none has visited, to the demoniac whom none has calmed, to the fallen whom none has lifted, to the leper whom none has touched, to the bereaved whom none has comforted, to the opening of the prison to them that are bound. Then shall I have the birthright of the first born, then shall I have the blessing of the Mighty God of Jacob!

Christ of love, give me room in my heart for earth's little ones. I have room for the heights, but not the vales, of humanity; let me descend with Thee into the vale. I have been despising those to whom Thou speakest in parables. Remind me that it is Thou Who speakest in parables—that the crude image covers a faith Divine. . . . When I stand on the mount of Thy love, the height shall dissolve the difference between the great and the little ones.[12]

Son of Man, Who hast reached Thy highest glory in the inability to save Thyself, grant me this enlarging powerlessness.[13]

It is wonderful how the Lord provided for His devoted servant. Dr. Matheson's unmarried sister was devoted to him and gave her life to make his as pleasant as possible, shielding him from unnecessary worries and troubles. His other two sisters also took care of him from time to time so that, despite his blindness, he considered his life a happy one. The young men who acted as his private secretaries were also indispensable to him, especially William Smith, who served Dr. Matheson the last ten years of his life.

George Matheson did not fear death, for he viewed the grave as but a gateway to glory:

Death is the gate to higher work and purer joys. Here on earth everything ripens except man. The fruit ripens every year. A longer season would make them no bigger and no better, but what man ever came to full maturity. Even in the most saintly there are faculties not fully developed, affections not applied to the highest objects. Are these never to ripen or do their highest work? Is there no sphere where the good and the gifted shall come to the perfection of their full power? The saints, as we term them, those who have grown in grace and knowledge, are as the plants of promise removed by death from this cold world to another, more congenial, in which they will grow in beauty and in strength, and find sweet exercise for each function. Life, long or short, is but a waiting to be born into a higher sphere, and death is the birth-angel.[14]

When Dr. Matheson took ill at sixty-six years of age, his doctor thought he would recover as he had a fine constitution. But his Master had other plans and called His servant home. With such a glorious view of his future Home, it is little wonder that those with him at his passing commented that he had indeed an "abundant entrance" into the realms above. This dear man who had traveled the road of descent all his life had found death but an ascent into the presence of his beloved Savior.

Jonathan Goforth
1859-1936

Jonathan Goforth

He Suffered the Loss of All Things

YOUNG Jonathan sat eagerly looking into the face of the minister as he listened to the earnest appeal. It seemed to him that the Rev. Cameron of the Presbyterian Church looked right at him as he pled for someone to yield to Christ. This momentous moment is told by himself:

> His words cut me deeply and I said to myself, "I must decide before he is through." But contrary to his usual custom, he suddenly stopped and began to pray. During the prayer, the devil whispered, "Put off your decision for another week." Then immediately after the prayer, Mr. Cameron leaned over the pulpit and with great intensity and fervor again pled for decisions. As I sat there without any outward sign except to simply bow my head, I yielded myself up to Christ.[1]

How complete was that yielding can be seen by his after-life, and also from the following, dictated to a daughter on his seventy-fifth birthday: "My conversion at eighteen was simple but so complete that ever onwards I could say with Paul, 'I am crucified with Christ; nevertheless I live; yet not I but Christ liveth in me; and the life which I now live in the flesh I live by the faith of the Son of God who loved me and gave Himself for me' (Gal. 2:20). Henceforth my life belonged to Him Who had given His life for me."

Fervent and whole-hearted as Jonathan Goforth had been in all his work, he now put the same diligence into serving Christ. He bewildered the staid old elders and caused a smirk on the faces of the young as he would stand at the church door giving out tracts. Very soon he started a church service in an old schoolhouse a little way from his home. He shocked the family by saying grace at the meals and also by asking for family worship.

A missionary call soon came to Jonathan through the reading of the life of Robert Murray McCheyne. His wife tells us how this came about.

> One Sunday afternoon Jonathan had occasion to go with horse and buggy to see his brother Will, whose farm lay some fifteen miles distant. He remained overnight and early Sunday morning started homeward. As he was leaving, Will Goforth's father-in-law, Mr. Bennett, a saintly old Scot, handed Jonathan a well-worn copy of *The Memoirs of Robert Murray McCheyne*, saying, "Read this, my boy, it'll do you good." Laying the book on the seat beside him the young man drove off.
>
> The day was one of those balmy, Indian summer days in October. Jonathan had not gone far when, remembering the book, he opened it and began to read as he drove slowly on. From the first page the message of the book gripped him. Coming to a clump of trees by the roadside, he stopped the horse and tethering it to a tree made a comfortable seat of dry leaves, and gave himself up to the *Memoirs*. Hour after hour passed unnoticed, so great was his absorption in what he was reading. Not till the shadows had lengthened did he awake to how time had passed. He rose and continued his journey, but in those quiet hours by the roadside, Jonathan Goforth had caught the vision and had made the decision which changed the whole course of his life.
>
> The thrilling story of McCheyne's spiritual struggles and victories, and his life sacrifices for the salvation of God's chosen people, the Jews, sank deep into his very soul. All the petty, selfish ambitions in which he had indulged vanished forever, and in their place came the solemn and definite resolve to give his life to the ministry.[2]

Rev. Cameron was so encouraged by the lad's dedication that he made arrangements to give him lessons in Latin and Greek in preparation for entrance into Knox College. His reading consisted of carefully chosen books which would help him in his future calling. But the Bible held first place, and to this sacred Book he gave two hours each morning before work.

A lovely farewell and a trip across the ocean will not make a missionary if the heart of a missionary has not been implanted by the Holy Spirit long before. God always prepares His servants in the school of hard knocks, and Jonathan was no exception to this rule. God had a peculiar and exceptional work for the new recruit to do abroad, but He wanted to show him the hollowness of much of the religion around him. It was to be through fiery ordeal that he was to learn to take his first disappointment.

This disappointment came to him in an unexpected way. The time had now come for the enthusiastic missionary candidate to enter Knox College in Toronto, but from the moment he entered the college, he was looked upon as extremely singular. The city youths, all ministerial or missionary candidates, despised Jonathan's country manners, and his home-made clothes became the object of much ridicule. Before him lay a lone road, yes, lone—even in a college like this. He was a misfit in the realms of earthly wisdom, because he was a citizen of another kingdom.

His wife describes his struggle one evening, after he had been subjected to much contempt: "That night he knelt with Bible before him and struggled through the greatest humiliation and the first great disappointment of his life. The dreams he had been indulging in but a few days before had vanished, and before him, for a time at least, lay a lone road. Henceforth he was to break an independent trail. It is not hard to see God's hand in this, forcing him out as it did into an independence of action which so characterized his whole after-life."

A classmate, Dr. Charles W. Gordon, describes Goforth at this time in a letter written many years later to Mrs. Goforth:

> My first impression of him was that he was a queer chap—a good fellow—pious—an earnest Christian but simple-minded and quite peculiar. . . . Jonathan's earnest devotion to his work—mission work down in the slums of St. John's Ward—seemed to me as rather quaint. . . . His dinner-table tales sometimes amused, at other times annoyed, his fellow students. His activities in the saving of the lost aroused in some a contempt for his simplicity. He became a subject for an "Initiation Ceremony"; hailed at midnight before his judges, students at Knox College, he was subjected, I learned, to indignities and warned against further breaches of good form by his tales of his "experiences with sinners."[3]

While most of his fellow students were interested only in the athletic and literary side of college life, rather than the uplifting of down-trodden and fallen men and women, Jonathan Goforth shared St. Paul's life's goal—"This one thing I do." This was to color his whole future life, but in order to fully understand this striking and decided personality, we shall have to remember that Jonathan came from a family of hardy settlers. His grandfather, John Goforth, was formerly from Yorkshire in England, and was one of the early pioneers who settled in Canada in 1846. Francis, one of his three sons, married Jane Bates of Irish descent. Jonathan was the seventh of eleven children, ten boys and one girl, and was born into the New London farm home on February 10, 1859.

Those were hard days for the settlers and doubtless the hardship the Goforth family endured did much to prepare that missionary son for pioneering in China under untold difficulties. Jonathan had to toil long hours on the farm which often interfered with his school life. But the disciplines of life were preparing the boy for his future vocation.

Meanwhile, he faithfully and joyously continued his work in the slums of Toronto, making calls from door to door, reading the Bible, and praying. Goforth was in God's training school, and slum work was but an introduction to the kind of labor that was to engage so much of his energy later in China. Someone has said that no missionary should go to the field without an experience in slum work. The transition is so vast between the civilized life and heathenism that many are totally unprepared for the cultural changes. Jonathan, however, was being well prepared, and in later years he had reason on several occasions to thank God for his former experiences in the slums of Toronto.

On one occasion, the principal of the college asked Goforth how many families he had visited in Toronto that summer. "Nine hundred and sixty," came the reply. "Well, Goforth," commented his Principal, "if you don't take any scholarships in Greek and Hebrew, at least there is one book that you're going to be well up in, and that is the book of Canadian human nature."

A few years experience in various kinds of mission work gave Jonathan further training. At one place there was no salary offered and faith was tested numerous times—another asset so needful for his future. The year previous to his sailing for China, the Presbyterian Church appointed him to visit churches in order to speak on behalf of missions abroad.

For some time, the question as to how and when Jonathan would go out to China remained unsettled. Then, amazingly, Knox Alumni wished to adopt him as their missionary, and the Presbyterian Church decided to plant a church in China, thus resolving the whole matter.

Jonathan, now twenty-eight, was ordained in October, 1887, and married in the same month. The remarkable way in which God brought Rosalind into his life is recounted in the following sketch of his wife's interesting life. They were now ready to start out on their long journey. The sea voyage was not exactly a pleasant one, for God does not coddle His finest called ones. On boarding the ship, they found that Rose was the only woman passenger. The ship's carpenter told them of his fear for the voyage as the captain had been seen so drunk he needed to be carried down to his cabin. The vessel had been repainted and renamed the Parthia so as to disguise her former notoriety as possessing a rolling pitch which had discouraged so many prospective travelers. Goforth's comment on the voyage was short and simple: "An ordinary water voyage; bad enough; sick all the way."

On their arrival in China, the first hurdle to be crossed was the language barrier. The months of tiresome study of the language is often a time of testing to the raw recruit anxious to get on the field and begin his evangelizing. Goforth soon discovered that his talents were not linguistic. His colleague, McGillivray, was soon racing ahead. The Chinese listening to them were quick to show their preference. The wonderful way in which God undertook for His chosen one is best told in his wife's words:

> In God's own mysterious way, He performed one of His wonders in answer to others' prayers. One day when Jonathan was about to leave for chapel, he said to his wife: "If God does not work a miracle for me with this language, I fear I will be an utter failure as a mission-

ary." For only a moment he looked the heartbreak that that would mean. Then picking up his Chinese Bible, he started off. Two hours later he returned.

"Oh, Rose," he cried, "it was just wonderful! When I began to speak, those phrases and idioms that would always elude me, just came readily and I could make myself understood so well that the men actually asked me to go on though Donald had risen to speak. I know the backbone of the language is broken. Praise the Lord!"

Mr. Goforth then made a full note of this in his diary. About two months later, a letter came from Mr. Talling (his former college roommate still in Knox) saying that on a certain evening after supper, a number of students decided to meet in one of the class rooms for prayer, "just for Goforth." The letter stated that the presence and power of God was so manifestly felt by all at that meeting, they were convinced Goforth must surely have been helped in some way. On looking up his diary, Mr. Goforth found the meeting for prayer by the students in Knox coincided with the experience recorded above.[4]

"We owe the grandeur of our lives to our tremendous difficulties," said Spurgeon. And so it was to prove in the lives of Rosalind and Jonathan Goforth, for the missionaries had been assigned North Honan as their field of labor for the Presbyterian Church of Canada. A letter from Hudson Taylor at this time to the new missionaries would have been daunting to less courageous pioneers, for it said, "We as a Mission have sought for ten years to enter that province of Honan from the south and have only just succeeded. . . . Brother, if you would enter that province, you must go forward on your knees."

Pioneer ventures have been a recorded history of lives laid down, repeated illness, not to speak of personal losses. Contending with diseases of the worst kind has to be encountered as these trailblazers live in unhygenic surroundings often with cholera or small pox raging. This is made even worse as medical aid and nearness to doctors are often denied. All this became the portion of the young Canadian couple who were bereaved of five of their children whom they left behind in kindly graves as they pressed ever onward. We have told, in the sketch of Rosalind Goforth, how they lost their valuable possessions by fire, but they were to lose, once more, all they had gathered together to make up another home. This time it was to be by flood which left furniture, curtains, and other items so moldy that they were considered of no value.

To make things even less comfortable, rumors had spread that these foreign devils had kidnapped little children, using their hearts and eyes for medicine which had been so effective in healing their diseases. Day followed day when their houses were invaded by as many as twenty men and women at a time. These came trooping to their compound to be shown all through their house and cellar where they overturned coal and boxes in order to find the bodies of the children the missionaries had supposedly killed. This search satisfied many. But to the missionaries' dismay, they later found articles missing which the women had tucked up their sleeves.

His biographer tells about it as it reached its climax: "The high-water mark in visitors received was reached one day in the fall of 1899, when 1,835 men passed through the house. On the same day, Mrs. Goforth received about 500 women." And Mr. Goforth comments, "I have often been receiving and talking to band after band of men in my study from morning right on till evening."

Trying days in extreme heat with strangers trooping through their house in constant streams meant inconvenience, weariness, and frustration. It was found, however, to be a wonderful means of getting the Gospel to these curious seekers.

Another peril to the Gospellers was the advice of older, experienced missionaries which could have meant years of stalemate had it been followed:

> "Do not attempt to speak of Jesus the first time when preaching to a heathen audience. The Chinese have a prejudice against the name of Jesus. Confine your efforts to demolishing the false gods and if you have a second opportunity you may bring in Jesus." Later, when telling his wife of the advice which had been given him, Mr. Goforth exclaimed with hot emphasis, "Never, never, never! The Gospel which saved the down and outs in the slums of Toronto is the same Gospel which must save Chinese sinners."

From the very first, when able to speak only in broken and imperfect sentences, Mr. Goforth preached to the Chinese Jesus Christ and Him crucified, and from the first, sinners were saved from the lowest depths of depravity. He based his messages always on some passage in the Word of God. Never was he known to stand before a Chinese audience without the open Bible in hand, constantly referring to it as "the written Word of the One true God."

In later years when asked by young missionaries as to the secret of his power in winning converts, his reply was: "Because I just give God a chance to speak to souls through His own Word. My only secret in getting at the heart of big sinners is to show them their need and tell them of a Savior abundantly able to save."[5]

The Boxer rebellion was soon to come and take its toll in many martyred missionaries. The Goforths and their children experienced hair-raising escapes as they made their way through angry mobs who cried out, "Kill them, kill them!" Jonathan's survival was a miracle, for he sustained a blow at the back of his neck which would have severed it had the instrument not been so blunt. His arm was gashed in three places, and yet they traveled on and on towards the coast, spending nights in whatever hide-out they could find. Only God could have sustained and brought them through this fiery ordeal so that they might continue their soul-winning efforts.

Goforth was nearing his forty-fifth milestone when a certain verse of Scripture, "Verily, verily, I say unto you, he that believeth in me, the works that I do shall he do also, and greater works than these shall he do," produced a strange restlessness in his soul. He could never be satisfied with just touching the fringes of the great work that lay before him. His soul burned with intensity. Could not the promise of "greater works" be fulfilled in his life? If this was God's Word, and it was, then why not expect a fulfillment of it?

Reports of the Welsh revival reached him about this time as well, encouraging his faith that if something could happen in Wales, it could happen also in China. At this point, an entirely new revelation came to Goforth. He read in the Scriptures of a powerful, divine Agent Who could work with him and produce the results that were promised. The work of the Holy Spirit fascinated Jonathan Goforth. He studied the Scriptures and was amazed to find how much the Bible spoke of the work that the Holy Spirit would do.

His wife feared that he was studying too deeply and finding him on his knees said, "Jonathan, are you not going too far in this? I fear you will break down!" He arose from his knees, put his hands on her shoulders and said sadly, "Oh, Rose, even you do not understand. I feel like one who has tapped a mine of wealth. It is so wonderful. If I could only get others to see it!"

Later, when he went out to preach on the ministry of the Holy Spirit, he felt a strange, new impetus in his labors, and noticed that there was a conviction that carried his words to the hearts of the hearers, producing what similar efforts had never previously been able to accomplish.

About this time, too, he was sent by a friend in India a booklet containing selections from Finney's Revival Lectures. As Goforth read these extracts from Finney, his emotions were deeply stirred. At last he said, "It simply means this: The spiritual laws governing a spiritual harvest are as real and tangible as the laws governing the natural harvest. . . . If Finney is right, and I believe he is, I am going to find out what these spiritual laws are and obey them no matter what the cost may be."

Goforth's message now was, "Not by might, nor by power, but by my Spirit." We quote what someone has said about his revival work at this time. "The cross burns like a living fire in the heart of every address." Goforth had gone up to Manchuria, comparatively unknown except within a narrow circle, but when he returned, the attention of the Christian world was focused upon him and his effort. He began meeting the calls which now came pouring in from all parts of China for revival meetings.

One of his colleagues writes thus about another effort at the same time:

What happened? Nothing more than God has promised from the beginning when the Holy Spirit is poured out—He will convict the world of sin. The church in Changte has been baptized by the Holy Spirit and cleansed and the greatest thought in the minds of all here now is, "Why did we so long despise His working and trust in other ways to build up His kingdom?"

. . . As Mr. Goforth's object in these meetings was not a revival among the heathen but among the Christians, it was necessary for us to call into the central station all who would come from the seven counties of this district. . . . On Monday morning, his text was: "I know thy works, that thou art neither cold nor hot." After the addresses, an opportunity was given for prayer. . . and thereupon ensued such a scene as never before I had witnessed nor again expect to see. A man started to pray but he had not said more than half a dozen words, when another, and then another joined in, and in a moment the whole company was crying aloud to God for mercy. . . . The pent-up emotions of a life-time seemed to be poured forth at that time. All the sin of the past was staring them in the face, and they were crying in anguish to God for mercy.

That which weighed most heavily on the consciences of all was that we had so long been grieving the Holy Spirit by not giving Him His rightful place in our hearts and in our work. While believing in Him we had not trusted in Him, to work in and through us. Now we believe, we have learned our lesson that it is "not by might, nor by power, but by my Spirit, saith the Lord of hosts." May we never forget that lesson.[6]

Meanwhile, in Canada, reports were circulating about Goforth and his revival movement. *The Presbyterian Record* and other papers created an interest. Some of the clergy declared that his methods were all out of keeping with Presbyterian procedure. Unaware of this criticism, Goforth went back on fire, full of hope that he might see a similar revival at home. Much time was given to prayer during the days preceding the General Assembly. Goforth arose in the Assembly and for twenty minutes pled for teachers, leaders, and professors to humble themselves before the Lord and see the outpouring of the Holy Spirit. This he held out as the only way to a revival; otherwise the church was certain to fail.

To Goforth's surprise there was a great deal of opposition. There were a few who welcomed his exhortation, but to many he was considered a fanatic. In later years, he learned that it was this speech before the Assembly that had caused him to be shunned and opposed. Only a few of the churches would welcome Jonathan into their pulpits. Where he did preach there were a few droppings. Had he lost the divine assistance he had known in China? We who read these pages believe that once again this man of God was experiencing what the great Example, Christ, experienced in His home town—"He could not do many mighty works because of their unbelief."

Once again Goforth returned to China only to meet many setbacks. When this wonderful revival had come, Goforth had expected the full support of his fellow-workers. He was disappointed in this. But it did not daunt him. New workers were not forthcoming; money for the spread of the Gospel was not so freely given from old sources. Goforth knew that God would raise up both men and money for a work that He Himself would direct—and He did.

Early one morning, Mr. Goforth was greatly agitated over a new rule passed by the Presbytery, curtailing some of his evangelistic efforts. His wife, in asking him if anything was wrong, received this answer: "Yes, I feel bound, hampered, hindered! Oh, that God would give me an opportunity before I pass on to demonstrate to missionaries and to the home Church what results would follow if we but give God a chance by broadcasting this wonderful message of salvation by every possible means in our power! I am convinced this simple Gospel story has never had a chance in China."

What was there about Dr. Goforth that could account for the phenomenal blessing that accompanied his labors? We might list a few reasons as gleaned from his biography:

1. It was his conviction that it was "not by might, nor by power, but by my Spirit, saith the Lord." He was convinced that the Holy

Spirit was available to anyone who, sensing their nothingness and helplessness, would depend solely upon God's Agent to help in such efforts.

2. Instead of an attitude of superiority, Goforth took a humble approach toward his Chinese helpers. When traveling, he discovered that they were at times seeking ease and comfort, so that instead of riding while they walked, he would refuse the ride and walk with them instead.

When he had finally built his new house, he asked God how he could use this means in the salvation of the Chinese. As we have described earlier, he opened his wife and himself to great inconvenience by allowing hordes of men and women to enter and be shown throughout.

3. Jonathan firmly believed that God could guide a person. Rosalind speaking of this said:

> Then, at this time, again we saw a wonderful indication of God's guiding and preventing hand over us, for every one of the five fields I have mentioned as having opened and then closed to us, had been completely evacuated of all missionaries and the work brought to a standstill, continuing so for a considerable time.

> Dr. Goforth believed firmly in the divine guidance through the agency of God's Holy Spirit. He made this the basis of his preaching and he sought to live thereby. When the invitation came to him to carry on special evangelistic meetings in other parts of China, many members of the Honan Mission urged upon him that his first duty was to Honan. He had been instrumental in founding the Mission—the work was great—the laborers few—he should remain and consolidate the work he had begun. The reason seemed weighty, but Dr. Goforth was convinced that it was the Spirit's guidance, and he remained firm in his purpose, although he came back at intervals to carry on work in his own field.[7]

4. Another reason for God's signal blessing was that Dr. Goforth was willing to work in weakness.

> Our little band gathered together and started for Manchuria by train—and what a weak band we were! The leader, an old man nearing

seventy, with a semi-invalid wife; a "Salvation Army lassie"—Miss Graham from New Zealand; a Dutch lady—Miss Annie Kok; and one young recruit, Rev. Alan Reoch, as yet struggling with the language. Little wonder, then, that a young missionary of a certain mission in Manchuria, on hearing of the personnel composing the Presbyterian Mission from Canada exclaimed, "Well, that sure is some Mission!" But, as it seemed to us later, our very weakness was an opportunity for our Almighty Lord and Captain to reveal what He could do.[8]

5. A further reason was that he refused to retire when illness and blindness overtook him:

God used the time of illness in Jonathan Goforth's life in the writing of a book. Miss Margaret Gay, an experienced nurse and a former worker in Honan, on hearing of Dr. Goforth's condition, canceled all her cases and gave herself to act as his night nurse. For months, with eyes bandaged, when able, Dr. Goforth recounted to Miss Gay, story after story as they later appeared in *Miracle Lives of China*. These stories Miss Gay took down in shorthand, and later handed them to Mrs. Goforth in a form that she could get ready for publication.[9]

6. His love for the Bible may be perhaps the most important reason for his astonishing results. We have already noticed that, as a new convert, Jonathan decided to give two hours in the early morning to his Bible and prayer. This habit was never abandoned even when pressure of work and the aging process might have caused him to diminish these priceless early morning hours of prayer. He went to the Word as a gold digger might resort to his mining. He considered it a great prize. "There were few moments during the day when absolute quiet reigned, yet never once was his wife able to recall his having shown impatience or express annoyance at the noise. . . . He always rose at five in summer and six in winter. Ten minutes were given to the daily dozen, and within half an hour of rising, he had started his intensive Bible study with pencil and notebook."

In Dr. Goforth's Chinese New Testament there was this statement: "October 18, 1932—Have read this Chinese New Testament sixty times."

Even after becoming blind, he had a Chinese read to him at least twelve chapters a day. His loyalty to the Bible as the Word of God and his defense of the fundamentals of the faith have been outstanding in his career.

> The question often asked was, "How did he, living the full life he did, manage to get so much time for Bible Study?" The answer to this is—by always rising early, having his Bible at hand, and using the extra minutes of opportunity as they came.
> To him the simple reading of it was a delight. It was sacred, divine. How often have I seen him, when taking up his Bible to read, first uncover his head and in an attitude of deepest reverence remain so a few moments before beginning his reading. In this simple act, we see the secret of his life. Before he crossed the border-land, he stated that he had read the Bible seventy-three times from cover to cover![10]

Because Goforth sacrificed work in order to make room for communion and Bible Study, thus seeking first the Kingdom of God, he found added to him an intercessor who was an invalid but who had prayed for him in some of his most trying moments.

"I cannot be at home in a world that crucified my Lord," said a godly saint who had doubtless known how difficult it is, save by compromise, to be subject to the pressures around without feeling ostracized. The following poem, which I have known for many years, is obviously written by one who is well aware of the danger of being squeezed into the world's mold and thus avoiding conflict.

> He has no enemies, you say?
> My friend, your boast is poor:
> He who hath mingled in the fray
> Of Duty, that the brave endure,
> Must have made foes. If he has none,
> Small is the work that he has done.
> He has hit no traitor on the hip;
> He has cast no cup from tempted lip;
> He has never turned the wrong to right,
> He has been a coward in the fight.
> —*Anon.*

The Joshuas and Calebs always are threatened with stones by the religious dwellers in ease. Jonathan Goforth was no exception. Goforth had not met with the greatest understanding from the Honan Presbytery, but he also found it necessary to resign his position with the Home Board in protest to the "higher criticism'" which had infected one of his hopeful converts, when sent to seminary. He observed that the same modernistic spirit was also invading newer recruits coming to North Honan. His understanding biographer says of this time:

> We have come to what I feel to be the most difficult point of this record. To be faithful to Jonathan Goforth's memory, the following facts must be given. For years, the teaching which was called "higher criticism" and "modernism" had been increasingly taught in the colleges of the homeland, and, as was inevitable, its reaction became more and more evident on the foreign field. Mr. Goforth was never one to mince words when deeply stirred on what he deemed, "a lowering of the standards of truth." Of that time we know not how to write. There was keen contention. I will give simply Goforth's answer to one word applied to him—"intolerant!"
>
> "Intolerant!" he exclaimed, "if you saw one undermining the foundation of a structure you, and others with you, had given the best of their lives to build, would it be intolerant to use every ounce of strength in combating the wrecker?"[11]

Fortunately the Board would not accept his resignation, but, though he continued to receive the same salary, he was denied additional funds so vital to expansion. How costly some of our decisions are! Three times previously they had lost their possessions, now the home they had built was required by the missionary taking his place in Honan. David's plea was to not offer to the Lord that which cost him nothing. Henceforth Goforth's future home was to be nomadic just at the time when old age and ill health would have demanded a more settled and comfortable abode. But at least he was free to open up new fields in Manchuria.

This venture led the Goforths further into a life of faith for financing such a large enterprise. An extract from a letter from Goforth to his Home Board is given:

> Our estimates for 1932-3 are cut to the lowest possible amounts to maintain any kind of efficiency and you will notice that not one dollar is down in the estimates for evangelists' salaries. . . . As long as the Lord of the Harvest gives me strength, I dare not stand still, but must extend the work. No matter how the work expands on present lines, the Home Church is not responsible for a single school, a single hospital, a single house, or a single foot of land. All the buildings are rented, and the year we cease to pay the rent, they revert to the owners. Up to the present, all evangelists used are paid by funds not raised by the Home Church; they are clearly told that when the funds fail, they return home. . . . At present there is a spiritual depression in the Home Church as well as a financial. Consequently there is a temporary inclination to walk by sight. We do sympathize with the Board on account of the deficit. . . .[12]

Many in these days do not believe in a personal devil. They feel it is superstitious to acknowledge his working in this world; but those in whom the Holy Spirit has taken His abode know the severe and very frequent attacks of Satan against them and their work.

Dr. Martyn Lloyd-Jones astutely comments: "I suggest that a belief in a personal devil and demon activities is the touchstone by which one can most easily test any profession of Christian truth today." If that be the case, then Dr. Goforth of China certainly passed that test.

While God abundantly blessed the work in Manchuria, the Goforths felt keenly the opposition of Satan at this time. Here they were with Dr. Goforth in his seventies, facing the loss of sight and the complete break-up of his work owing to severe cuts in his budget by the Home Board. "The devil is trying his best to wreck our mission," exclaimed Dr. Goforth, "but God is with us and he will bring us through!"

His wife comments further on that trying period of their lives:

> The events of that period brought Kipling's lines vividly to mind:

> If you can watch the things you gave your life to, broken
> And stoop and build 'em up with worn-out tools. . . .

> Preparations were at once made for the break-up of our party. . . .
> But before breaking up, the following which is a brief extract from a
> letter dictated by Dr. Goforth, was dispatched to the Home Board:
> ". . . We have just received word of the outcome of the Council
> recently held at Szepingkai. One item will give you some idea of the
> dismay caused by what has been decided at this Council. Twenty-four
> dollars per month, *Mexican*, is all that is being allowed for Szepingkai's
> main center and its fourteen outstations. To save money, it is even
> being suggested that we dismiss our good trustworthy gatekeeper, a
> man who has been with us for four years and does not only the hun-
> dred and one things required of one in his position, but often takes
> charge of the street-chapel and preaches to those who come. . . . It
> simply means that we cannot carry on the work unless we use our own
> depleted salary to meet the extra expenses. We are determined that if
> we have to spend our last dollar, the Lord's work must go on."[13]

Death visited this warrior of many battles with a gentle passing. Jonathan had gone through tribulation most of his life to find
that his exit into eternal life and the Savior's presence took place
swiftly and peacefully. He had taken a service for his son, Frederick,
the night before and refused refreshments at the close saying he
had slight indigestion.

Rose arose from bed in the morning and believing her husband yet asleep, returned later to find he had taken flight in a most
relaxed manner, passing from his earthly sphere into glory just
after Rose had risen. The Master had come and found His faithful
servant still giving out portions to his fellow Christians. I am sure
His "well done" was given to a man who, putting his hand to the
plough had never turned back for nearly half a century.

Rosalind Goforth
1864-?

Rosalind Goforth

A SKETCH of Jonathan Goforth, a Caleb who wholly followed the Lord, would not be complete without a companion sketch of Rosalind, his undaunted wife. Her story has many humorous side lights as she sought to ever keep step with her aggressive life-partner. Never flinching, she traveled with him until the end of his long life, over almost impossible roads, gave birth to eleven children, and faced angry mobs as well as friendly Chinese inquirers. She wrote his excellent biography, choosing the splendid highlights of his life, and showing a willingness to let her readers know of her mistakes and of her husband's kindly reprimands; this openness can be a great help to many another. We have retained her own words as much as possible, for we could not hope to improve on her talents as a spiritual writer.

It was on May 6th, 1864, in Kensington Gardens, London, that Rosalind entered the world to begin her interesting journey. Seven brothers and four sisters came into the nursery to receive the latest addition to the Bell-Smith family. The fragile bundle of life so pink in its appearance occasioned the suggestion that she be named Rose. As she grew into girlhood, it soon became evident that she had inherited her father's artistic talent, but she was strong-willed as well as gifted. Rosalind tells, in her autobiography, how her mother proved well able to discipline her imperious and passionate twelfth child:

> But mother understood! How often when others were clamoring that I should receive a severe chastisement for some grievous misdemeanor, mother would draw me close to her, and, as I sobbed out for

her alone to hear, "Oh mother, I do, I do want to be good; I do want to be good," I could feel her arms draw me closer, as she whispered: "Some day, Rosey, some day, it will all come right."

Then would follow the punishment, but in mother's way, which was to have me to sit alone in the quiet drawing-room while I memorized Bible verses to suit the offense. . . .

On one occasion when I had hurt seriously the arm of a schoolmate (she really had as bad a temper as I), my punishment was to master perfectly the entire "love chapter." I can even now recall the fear that came upon me when learning some of those searching passages giving the consequences, for example, of telling a lie, this when I had been caught in deception.

When about eight, possibly nine, years of age, my parents were puzzled as to how to break me of the habit of leaving tasks unfinished and slipping out to play, for I would much rather be playing with a neighbor's baby, than drawing beside my father's easel. One day, mother took me alone and, opening her Bible at the parable of the talents, had me read the whole passage. Though I cannot recall her words, a lasting impression was made upon me as she made vividly plain that someday God would require me to give an account of the talents he had given me. This plan of mother's in using God's Word did help, for from that time on I tried to apply myself to drawing and other lessons.[1]

Rose's family moved to Canada when she was only three. As the years passed, she would sometimes accompany her mother to Montreal, and after a visit to the market, her mother would say, "Now, child, we will go into the cathedral; I need quiet." She would then make her way to Notre Dame Cathedral where, upon entering, she would politely acknowledge the priest and pass on to a seat, where she would kneel in perfect stillness for an hour or more. This greatly impressed the child as to the importance of prayer in her mother's life.

At eleven years of age, an event occurred which proved a decisive factor in her future. She describes it vividly:

Revival meetings were being held in the Cross Sunday School. One evening, I was allowed to accompany my oldest sister to the meeting. We sat in one of the front seats. The leader, Mr. Sandham, took as his text John 3:16 and spoke with great tenderness of the love of God. As he repeated again and again the words, "God loves you," my whole soul responded with gratitude and love. And when he asked all those who wished to take Jesus Christ as their Lord and Master, fear of my sister and others kept me from rising.

That night I sobbed and prayed for hours. At last I promised the Lord that if He would let me live until the next evening, I would confess Him. The following evening, I went to the meeting so full of what I was going to do (I had told no one) that I could afterwards remember nothing of what preceded the call for decisions. Mr. Sandham had the invitation to stand only partly out when I was on my feet and remained standing so long that he had to sign for me to sit down! All the while I was standing my sister was tugging at my dress. On the way home, I was told how foolish it was for me to stand as I had, that I was too young to understand. But I knew Christ had received me; that I belonged to Him. In the years to come, this defi- nite assurance of acceptance saved me many, many times from de- spair. And oh the joy of that "first love"! Would it had never grown cold! . . .

The autumn of 1882 found us again settled in Toronto when I at once entered the Art School. The period of three years that followed was a period of great unrest in my life. While I loved my art, for it was born in me, yet there was always the inner, secret longing for definite Christian service. I came to pray daily that a door might be opened for such.[2]

Rosalind's prayer was answered; that door was opened, but not before her Master had put her through His school of suffering. Her father had passed away peacefully two years after their return to Toronto, but not before obtaining the promise of his wife and eldest son to send Rosalind to England in order to finish her art education. However, a high Authority had other plans. Those plans were lived out in the fiery furnace of affliction. The following ex- cerpt from Rose's autobiography tells how the bonds that had tied her to art were burst asunder.

Early in February I was taken ill with inflammatory rheumatism. This was the third serious attack. For days my life hung in the balance. I was only half conscious and unable to move or be moved. Every joint in my body seemed on fire. Some weeks before, I had memorized the hymn, the first verse of which is:

How sweet the name of Jesus sounds
In a believer's ear;
It soothes his sorrows, heals his wounds,
And drives away his fears.

Words fail me to describe what that hymn meant to me through those days of agony. The words fresh in mind came without effort. While at times the whole six verses would come as soothing balm, it was the message of the first two lines of the last verse that brought to me the irresistible call to service. The words,

I would Thy boundless love proclaim
With every fleeting breath,

seemed burned into my soul. I came out of that valley of suffering determined to pray myself loose from the things that were forcing me to follow other than the path of Christian service.[3]

Romance usually comes to every young person, and God brought Jonathan Goforth into Rosalind's life in a remarkable and providential manner. Young Goforth had been previously attached to Charlotte Macleod, who was leader of the girls in the old log schoolhouse of West Missouri, while he held the same position with the boys. But Charlotte was Baptist while Jonathan was Presbyterian. This denominational difference was something that Charlotte found it impossible to reconcile, and it kept her from becoming his wife.

How Rosalind discovered her consecrated missionary is best told in her own words:

In the early part of 1885, when still in my twentieth year I began to pray that if the Lord wanted me to live the married life, he would lead me to one wholly given up to Him and to His service. I wanted no other. One Sunday in June of that year, a stranger took the place of the Honorable S. H. Blake, our Bible Class teacher. This stranger, Mr. Henry O'Brien, came to me about the hymns, as I was organist.

Three days later, two parties were crossing the lake on the same boat, one an artists' picnic, bound for the Niagara Falls; the other bound for the Niagara-on-the-Lake Bible Conference. I was with the former group, but my heart was right with the others who were evidently having a wonderful time of spiritual conference. That evening, all returned on the same boat with the addition of a Conference group who had crossed on the midday boat.

I was sitting in the artist circle, beside my brother F. M. Bell-Smith, when Mr. Henry O'Brien touched me saying, "Why, you are my organist of Sunday last! You are the very one I want to join us in the Mission next Sunday. We are to have a workers' meeting and tea, and I would like you to meet them all." I was on the point of saying this was impossible when my brother whispered, "You have no time. You are going to England." Partly to show him I could do as I pleased—what a trifle can turn the course of a life—I said to Mr. O'Brien, "Very well; expect me on Saturday."

As Mr. O'Brien turned to leave, he spied and called to one who looked to me to be a very shabby fellow, whom he introduced as "Jonathan Goforth, our city missionary." I forgot the shabbiness of his clothes, however, for the wonderful challenge in his eyes!

The following Saturday found me in the large, square, workers' room of the Toronto Mission Union. Chairs were set all round the walls, but the center was empty. Just as the meeting was about to begin, Jonathan Goforth was called out. He had been sitting across the corner from me with several people between. As he rose he placed his Bible on the chair. Then something happened which I could never explain, nor try to excuse. Suddenly I felt literally impelled to step across, past four or five people, take up the Bible and return to my seat. Rapidly I turned the leaves and found the book worn almost to shreds in part and marked from cover to cover.

Closing the book, I quickly returned it to the chair, and returning to my seat, I tried to look very innocent. It had all happened within a few moments, but as I sat there, I said to myself, "That is the man I would like to marry!"

That very day, I was chosen as one of a committee to open a new mission in the East end of Toronto, Jonathan Goforth being also on the same committee. In the weeks that followed, I had many opportunities to glimpse the greatness of the man which even a shabby exterior could not hide. So when, in that autumn he said, "Will you join your life with mine for China?" my answer was, "Yes," without a moment's hesitation.

But a few days later when he said, "Will you give me your promise that always you will allow me to put my Lord and His work first, even before you?" I gave an inward gasp before replying, "Yes, I will, always." For was not this the very kind of man I had prayed for? (Oh, kind Master, to hide from Thy servant what that promise would cost!)

A few days after my promise was given, the first test in keeping it came. I had been (woman-like) indulging in dreams of the beautiful engagement ring that was soon to be mine. Then Jonathan came to me and said, "You will not mind, will you, if I do not get an engagement ring?" He then went on to tell with great enthusiasm of the distributing of books and pamphlets on China from his room in Knox. Every cent was needed for this important work. I listened and watched his glowing face. The vision I had indulged in of the beautiful engagement ring vanished.[4]

There were a few hurdles for the young woman to jump before she was free to marry and enter Christian service. Smooth sailing gives way to stormy passages when there is a Divine purpose for the voyager. Arthur Mathews of the China Inland Mission speaks in a recorded sermon of how his call to China (Burma) was withstood. The sermon was named, "The Thing Spoken Is The Thing Attacked." Rosalind's call had been clear, but it was to suffer attack from an unexpected quarter.

In view of her promise to her dying husband, Rosalind's mother took stern measures to hinder her daughter's marriage. She had become suspicious when Jonathan constantly saw Rosalind home from the Mission, and finally objected.

Mother came to me and said sternly, "This slum work is to cease at once. You are to get ready and leave for England without delay!"

I replied quietly, but firmly, "Mother, it is too late; I promised Jonathan Goforth last night to be his wife and to go to China!"

Poor mother! She almost fainted! It is not necessary to give the details of the week that followed. Suffice it to say, Mother gave me the choice of obeying father's dying wish or leaving home. For six weeks, I stayed with a brother in a distant city. Then came a letter from my sister pleading with me to return, as mother was sobbing day and night and seemed failing fast.

On reaching home, I was shocked at the change in Mother. She would not speak to me and seemed broken-hearted. My distress was now very great. Could it be God's will for me to break my mother's heart? At last, one day, as I listened to her pacing her bedroom floor, weeping, I could stand the strain no longer and determined to find out God's will so plainly I could make no mistake. Going down to the parlor, where the large family Bible rested on a small davenport or desk, I stood for a moment crying to the Lord for some word of light. Then I opened the Bible at random, and the first words my eye lit on were: "Ye have not chosen me, but I have chosen you, and ordained you, that ye should go and bring forth fruit."

I knew at once God was speaking His will to me through these words, and in an instant the crushing burden was gone. Running to mother's room, I begged her to hear what I had to say. Unwillingly, she unlocked the door and stood while I told her of my prayer and answer. For a moment only she hesitated, then with a cry I could never forget, she threw her arms about me, saying, "Oh my child, I can fight against you, but I dare not fight against God." From that moment till her death, eighteen months later, mother's heart was entirely with me in the life I had chosen.[5]

The story of the many difficulties to be overcome before being finally accepted for the field of China is told in *Goforth of China*, Rosalind's biographical sketch of her husband. Her marriage, their acceptance by the Presbyterian Mission, his ordination, and the great difficulties in traveling to China, are also related.

We do wish, however, to include here the method in which God subdued the high-tempered, strong-willed missionary to Himself along with the story of how she experienced a deeper sense of her need which drove her to Christ and His full salvation. It is both fascinating and touching to read of how Rosalind came to learn how to accept the loss of endearing things and how her dedicated husband was the means of lovingly teaching her God's purposes in these disciplinary acts. Let us look at some of these invaluable lessons the young missionary learned in life's school.

She Learns How to Rightly Evaluate *Things*

It may seem a ruthless providence for a young missionary bride, facing a culture so different and circumstances so strange, to experience losses at the very start. While language study was proceeding, a rented premises had been obtained for the new missionaries. She tells the story in the third person:

> While the Goforths sat at dinner, screams and shouts were heard. Running outside, they found the bedroom at the farther end of the house was on fire. The old, thatched roof, dry as timber, was ablaze and already beginning to drop fire below. Again and again Goforth entered the burning rooms. The first thing to be secured were his beloved Bible and a valise containing the money. As he returned for more things, his panic-stricken wife grasped the valise and ran for the road, thinking it to be the safest place. In her agitated state she was unconscious of the hundreds of eyes watching eagerly for a chance to secure the valise. Fortunately, Goforth missed it before it was snatched from her. Running to his wife as she stood dazed by the roadside, he said sternly, "Pull yourself together and don't give way to panic! Do you not know the Chinese will steal?" It was the best thing for her for it brought her to her senses and from then on she was quite calm.
>
> Returning to the court, where the fire could be seen through the open doors, it was not a pleasant sight to watch wedding presents, pictures (one of them of her father painted by himself from a mirror), and other precious home things being licked up by the flames, but so it was. Practically everything of real value to them was burned. Later, Goforth tried to comfort his wife by saying, "My dear, do not grieve so. After all, they are just things."
>
> The fire meant little more to Goforth than a temporary hindering of his language study, for his optimism remained as unshadowed and his radiant cheerfulness as helpful as if it had not occurred. To his wife, it meant the burning of the bridges behind her as far as art was concerned and it meant also the dawn of personal responsibility toward the souls of her Chinese sisters.[6]

She Learns That the Missionary Must Be Her Message

The young mother in her mid-twenties welcomed her firstborn with delight; but her stay on earth was to be brief, for the heat, the travel in unhygienic conditions, and calling at inns took its toll and little Gertrude took up her abode in a friendlier atmosphere. As the young father traveled miles to bury their little one, the mourning mother tells her own story:

> One evening, as I lay on a couch beside a paper window, through which every sound could be heard, I was drinking to its dregs the cup of sorrow. Little Gertrude, our first born, had died that morning. The father was on his way to a distant station taking the precious remains for burial.
>
> Two Chinese women seated themselves outside the window. I could not help hearing what they said. They were of course, quite unconscious of my closeness to them. At first they talked with much kindness and sympathy of the event that had just taken place. Then began a most amazing and searching dissection (no better word can express it) of my life and character. We had been told the Chinese were keen judges of character. But this was more. It revealed a surprisingly high conception of a Christian missionary! Incidents with the servants which I had thought trivial, such as a stern rebuke, a hasty word or gesture, were all given their full value.
>
> During the process of dissection, they did, however, find some good points. One said, "She speaks our language well and is a zealous preacher." The other admitted, "And she does love us. But its her impatience, her quick temper!" Then came what struck me as a blow, "If she only would live more as she preaches!"
>
> At first I was so angered I could have gone out and given them a piece of my mind but no, I could not, for it was all too true. It was this fact that cut so deeply. Then there came the remembrance of how I had hoped and expected by giving up all, even my money, before leaving Canada for China, my disposition would change. I saw my mistake! As that last hard word was heard, "If only she would live more as she preaches," I fled to my room. I had heard enough. It was useless to stay in China and simply preach Christ and not live Christ even before our servants.
>
> Two days later my husband returned to find a doubly crushed and broken wife. Oh, what a comforter and help he was. For many days I walked softly, but the lesson had to be relearned many times. As I look back on that sad, searching experience, I can see clearly it was all a step higher in my life, as it was then, just a struggling overcomer, but an overcomer—a climber up life's mountain side.[7]

She Learns how Much She Should Give God

Another valuable lesson was taught this young wife so new to deeper spiritual lessons. Again it is written in the third person.

About the end of April, Goforth gave his wife her first lesson in real giving. Coming to her with his open account book in hand, he said, "I have been going carefully into our accounts and I find we have given a tithe of one year's salary already and we have been married just six months. What would you suggest about it?"

Now his wife had not been accustomed to tithing in her parents' home, and had thought it very generous of her husband to tithe their salary. She hesitated somewhat, however, before replying. "If we have already given a tithe of our year's salary, I suppose we need not give any more till the end of the year."

"Do you really feel we should do so?" Jonathan replied gravely, rather taken aback. "To me it seems right when the Lord has done so much for us that we should just close the account to date, and begin again."

This he did. So that year a fifth was given. This was but the first lesson of a progressive course in giving, for as the years passed, his wife became accustomed to a half, and on till only sufficient of their income for pressing needs was kept.

Though very sacred to the writer, the following incident is given which occurred just a month before Jonathan Goforth passed beyond the need for earthly finances. He was resting on a couch, waiting for a call to a meeting. His wife saw he was thinking keenly about something. Stepping to his side, she said laughingly: "Jonathan, I believe I can read your thoughts!"

"Nonsense," he answered. "But say on."

"You are planning how much of next month's salary you can safely give away without leaving us quite destitute!"

His hearty laugh rang out as he rose, "Well, my dearest, you are not far wrong!" he replied.[8]

She Learns About the Right Expenditure of Time

Among the young recruits arriving from the homeland were a Mr. and Mrs. X. Mr. X was a man with a college record equal to that of

Donald McGillivray—a gold medalist, a fluent speaker, but also a clever mechanic, especially along the line of carpentry.

When visiting Mrs. X, Goforth's wife often looked with envious eyes at the many clever conveniences X had made for his wife. One day she determined to coax her husband into making similar things for her. Going to him she said, "Now, Jonathan, don't you think you could leave your work for a little and do some carpentry for me like Mr. X does for his wife?"

"My dear, Rose," he replied, "don't ask this of me. There are fine Chinese carpenters who could do all you want far better than I and would be thankful for the job. Besides, I have determined never to spend my time on what Chinese can do, for my work is to preach or prepare to preach the Gospel that will save souls. You know, 'This one thing I do' is my motto. So, my dear, get the best carpenter going. Have him do all you require and I will foot the bill."

She went away only almost persuaded, but years later, she acknowledged how that many times she had thanked God for giving her a husband always consistent in putting "first things first." This trait in him many times helped her to bear more bravely her share of life's burdens.[9]

She Learns Obedience Through Tragedy

Rosalind and her five children were on furlough after the terrible Boxer Rebellion, when word reached her that her husband wished her to proceed once again to China, where he promised to meet her on her arrival. But Jonathan lay ill at a distance of a thousand miles with typhoid fever when his wife and children finally docked at Shanghai. After a few weeks of recovery, her husband, buoyant as ever, met her with a plan which first startled and then dismayed her. He wished her to travel to a new area where families were being visited by that deadly smallpox disease.

Perhaps it is small wonder that this thirty-eight-year-old mother should quail at the prospect of exposing her children to such a scourge when one considers that she had already lost four. Preferring to quietly settle in their home at Changte, she actually refused her husband's request.

They arrived at Changte on Saturday evening, but by Sunday morning their son, Wallace, had contracted the worst form of Asian dysentery, and for two weeks husband and wife battled for his life. We quote Rosalind's own words as to this ordeal.

For two weeks we literally fought for the child's life during which time my husband whispered to me gently: "O Rose, give in, before it is too late!" But I only thought him hard and cruel, and refused. Then, when Wallace began to recover, my husband packed up and left on a tour *alone*.

The day after he left, my precious baby Constance, almost one year old, was taken ill suddenly, as Wallace had been, only much worse. From the first, the doctors gave practically no hope. The father was sent for. Constance was dying when he arrived. We had laid her on a cot in the middle of my husband's study. Our faithful friend, Miss Pyke, knelt on one side. My husband knelt next to Constance, and I beside him. The little one was quietly passing, all was still, when suddenly I seemed to apprehend in a strange and utterly new way the love of God— as a *Father*. I seemed to see all at once, as in a flash, that *my heavenly Father could be trusted to keep my children!* This all came so overwhelmingly upon me, I could only bow my head and say, "Oh God, it is too late for Constance, but I will trust you. I will go where you want me to go. But keep my children!"

Oh, the joy that came and peace—so when my husband turned to me saying, "Constance is gone"—I was ready and comforted, knowing that her life had not been in vain. Our little Constance's remains were laid beside her two sisters' graves on her birthday, October 13, 1902.[10]

She Learns Protection Only In The Pathway of Duty

Instead of settling down in our comfortable home at Changte, I at once began preparations for the new life of itinerating with my husband. In the years that followed, weeks, even months, at a time were given to aggressive Evangelism in the larger centers of our field. It was indeed, a wonderful life in which to learn what a faithful Lord could and would do when all human props failed. It was not, by any means, an easy life—this traveling about from place to place with our remaining children, in constant contact with people who had no idea of sanitation: living in native compounds. But as I now recall those years, they seem among the happiest and certainly the most fruitful of my life. True, there were times when I was tempted to give up, but the Lord was ever present to encourage and sustain; and, oh, how much I owed to my patient, faithful, ever-cheerful husband. . . .

It was a wonderful life! Sometimes when letters would reach us from the Homeland expressing pity for us, how my husband would laugh as I read them to him! "Pity," he would say, "why this is the most glorious life possible!"[11]

One summer at our women's conference, made up entirely of women missionaries, married and single, a woman rose and said (as near as I can quote from her words):

"We mothers have heard with mixed feelings of Mrs. Goforth's going with her husband on his country tours and of her taking her children with her. I should like to ask Mrs. Goforth a question, in the name of other mothers, as well as myself, who want to do God's will—but we do fear for our children. My question is: 'Have your children suffered as the result of such a life, for we hear five of your children have died?'"

Rising, I replied: "I am most thankful for the opportunity to answer this question. The five children who have gone before all died *before* I began the touring life. Since I began that life, two children have been given us. Further, I have found the children happier and healthier than before. I have found it possible to give actually more time to them than before, for the time necessarily given to keeping up a foreign house may, when outside, be given to the children. I can truly say I know of no harm that has come to any during these eight or nine years of that life. Not one has contracted any infectious disease and, best of all, God has set His seal upon this plan of work by giving a harvest of souls everywhere we have gone."[12]

She Learns That Losing One's Temper Is Costly

As we have seen, the Goforths opened their home to curious Chinese which, though exceedingly annoying, still gave a unique opportunity for the missionaries to mingle with their foreign friends and give the Gospel to them.

The large Chinese sleeves of the Chinese women made lovely hiding places for Rosalind's scissors, pieces of pattern, or whatever lay ready to conceal. Listen to her vivid and humorous account of how, one day, her aggravation reached its limits:

> One day my husband taught me a lesson I could never forget. (He was really a wonderful disciplinarian!) The day had been an unusually strenuous one, and I was very tired. Toward evening a crowd of women burst open the living-room door and came trooping in before I had time to meet them outside. One woman set herself out to make things unpleasant. She was rough and repulsive and, well, just indescribably filthy.
>
> I paid no attention to her except to treat her as courteously as the rest. But when she put both hands to her nose, saying loudly, "Oh, these foreign devils, the smell of their home is unbearable!" my temper rose in a flash and, turning on her with anger, I said, "How dare you speak like that! Leave the room!" The crowd, sensing a storm, fled. I heard one say, "That foreign devil woman has a temper just like ours!"
>
> Now, I had not noticed that the door of my husband's study was ajar, nor did I know that he was inside, until, as the last woman disappeared, the door opened and he came forward, looking solemn and stern. "Rose, how could you so forget yourself?" he said. "Do you realize that just one such incident may undo months of self-sacrificing, loving service?"
>
> "But, Jonathan," I returned, "you don't know how she —."
>
> But he interrupted, "Yes, I do: I heard all. You certainly had reason to be annoyed; but were you *justified,* with all that is hanging in the balance and God's grace sufficient to keep you patient?"
>
> As he turned to re-enter his study, he said, *"All I* can say is *I am disappointed!"*
>
> Oh, how that last word cut me. I deserved it, yes, but, oh, I did so want to reach up to the high ideals he had. A tempestuous time followed alone in our inner room with my Lord. As I look back now, it was all just one farther step up the rocky hillside of life—just climbing![13]

She Learns How to Make Time for Communion

How many a young mother of children has found it difficult to rise in the morning in order to commune with God and gather strength for the day, for when they rise, they find that the children waken as well! Many of us have experienced similar difficulties as did Rosalind Goforth. Listen to her experience.

A devoted Christian missionary, Mrs. S., was holding a series of special meetings for our Christian women at Changte. On one occasion, this dear woman, who had no children, told me that I could never have the peace and joy I longed for unless I rose early and spent from one to two hours with the Lord in prayer and Bible Study.

I longed intensely for God's best—for all He could give me, not only to help me live the true Christian life but also for peace and rest of soul. So I determined to do what Mrs. S. had advised.

The following morning, about half-past five o'clock, I slipped as noiselessly as possible out of bed (my husband had already gone to his study). I had taken only a step or two when first one and then another little head bobbed up; then came calls of "Mother, is it time to get up?"

"Hush, hush, no, no," I whispered as I went back, but too late; baby had wakened! So of course the morning circus began an hour too soon.

But I did not give up easily. Morning after morning I tried rising early for the morning watch, but always with the same result. So I went back to the old way of just praying quietly—too often just sleeping! Oh, how I envied my husband, who could have an hour or more of uninterrupted Bible Study; but I could not. This led me to form the habit of memorizing Scripture, which became an untold blessing to me. I took advantage of odd opportunities on cart, train, or when dressing, always to have a Bible or Testament at hand so that in the early morning I could recall precious promises and passages of Scripture.[14]

She Learns Submission

Our children were all away at school. We were together carrying on aggressive evangelism at a distant out-station. The room given to us was dark and damp, with the usual mud floor. The weather had turned cold, and there was no place where one could get warm. I caught a cold. It was not a severe one, but enough to make me rather miserable.

The third or fourth day, when the meetings were in full swing and my organ was taking an attracting part, I became possessed by a great longing to visit my dearly loved friend, Miss H., some hours run south on the railway. But when I told my husband what I had in mind, he strongly objected and urged against my going. I would not listen, even when he said my going would break up at least the women's work. But I was determined to go and ordered the cart for the trip to the railway.

As the cart started and I saw my husband's sad, disappointed, white face, I would have stopped, but I wanted to show him I must have my way *sometimes!*

Oh, what a miserable time I had till my friend's home in Weihuifu was reached! Miss H. gave one glance at my face and exclaimed: "Whatever is the matter, Mrs. Goforth! Are you ill?"

My only answer was to break down sobbing. Of course, I could not tell her why. Miss H. insisted on putting me to bed, saying I was ill! She made me promise to remain there until after breakfast.

The following morning, while waiting for breakfast, I opened my Testament and started to memorize, as usual, my three verses. Now it happened I was at that time memorizing the Epistle to the Ephesians and had reached the fifth chapter down to the twenty-first verse. The twenty-second, the first of the three to be memorized that morning, read: *"Wives, submit yourselves unto your husbands as unto the Lord."*

I was, to say the least, startled! Somehow I managed to get this bravely memorized. Then going on to the twenty-third verse, these words faced me: "For the husband is the head of the wife, even as Christ is the head of the church: and he is the savior of the body."

For a moment a feeling of resentment, even anger, arose. I could not treat this word as a woman once did, putting it aside with the remark: "That is where Paul and I differ." I believed the Epistle to the Ephesians was inspired, as any portion of Scripture was. How could I dare cut out this one part to which I was unwilling to submit?

How I managed to memorize that twenty-third verse, I do not know, for all the while a desperate mental struggle was on. Then came the twenty-fourth verse: "Therefore as the church is subject unto Christ, so let the wives be to their own husbands in everything."

I could not memorize further: my mind was too agitated. "It just comes to this," I thought, "Am I willing, FOR CHRIST'S SAKE, to submit my will (in all but matters of conscience) to my husband?" The struggle was short but intense. At last I cried, **"For Christ's sake, I yield!"**

Throwing a dressing gown about me, I ran to the top of the stairs and called to my friend, "When does the next train go?"

"In about half an hour," she replied, "but you couldn't catch it and have your breakfast."

"Never mind; I'm going to get that train!"

My friend insisted on accompanying me to the station; we ate as we almost ran. With what joy I at last found myself traveling northward!

On reaching my destination, imagine my surprise to find my husband, with a happy twinkle in his eye, standing on the platform! "Why, Jonathan," I cried, "How did you know I was coming?"

His reply was simply a happy, "Oh, I knew you would come."

Later I told my husband frankly all I had passed through. What was the result? From that time, he gave me my way as never before, for does not verse twenty-five of the chapter quoted go on to say: "Husbands, love your wives, even as Christ loved the Church, and gave Himself for it." A new realization of the need of yieldedness came to us both, which has had blessed results in our home life.[15]

Rosalind has shared with us her many failures, but the sketch would not be complete unless we added her record of victory. We are so happy she has left this as a legacy to encourage us that in Christ there are inexhaustible supplies of grace to cover any weakness we may have inherited or accumulated through the years.

The experience I am about to record . . . was written and published over twenty years ago but is such a vital part of my life's story that it cannot be withheld from these pages.

On our first arrival home, many requests came for my husband to take meetings. When it became known that he could not, I was urged to take his place. But the months of ceaseless overland travel through Inland China with my husband, who was evidently breaking, the nursing, and the anxiety, had all told on me. I felt physically worn, spiritually dead, mentally numb. But deep in my heart I craved for some fresh spiritual blessing, for fresh vision that might enable me to speak once more out of an overflowing heart. . . .

We had been but a short time at the Rest Home when a friend carried me off, insisting that I needed a rest. She took me to Niagara-on-the-Lake, where a Bible Conference was being held. . . . The following morning we gathered under some trees by the auditorium, before the meeting. . . .

A short time passed. Suddenly there came an impelling to enter the auditorium. I obeyed, but the place being full, I walked forward and finally found a seat immediately in front of the pulpit. The speaker was just beginning his address. He was a stranger, but from almost his first sentence his message gripped me.

He drew simply but vividly, first a picture of an ordinary all-too-common Christian life. If he had drawn the picture from my everyday life experience, he could not have given it other than he did. Sometimes on the mountain-top with visions of God and His mighty power; then the sagging, the dimming of vision, coldness, discouragement, even definite disobedience and a time of down-grade experience. Again through some sorrow or trial, there would come a return and seeking of the Lord, with again the higher Christian experiences. In a word, an up and down life of intermingled victory and defeat.

The speaker then asked all who truly sought for God's highest and best, yet who knew the picture he had drawn was true of their Christian life and experience, to hold up their hands. Being in the front seat and realizing many behind knew who I was, and that they thought of me as a "good missionary," I kept my hand down. It was too humiliating to acknowledge that picture as representing me! But the Spirit of God strove with me. "If you keep your hand down you are a hypocrite! If you truly want God's best, humble yourself." So up went my hand.

Then, the speaker drew another picture: it was the Christian life as God had not only planned it for His children, but had made abundant provision for their living it. He described it as a life of victory, not defeat, of peace and trust, not struggle and worry. All through his address, I kept thinking, "Yes, its wonderful, but I've tried so often and failed, I doubt if it is possible."

Then the speaker ended by urging us to go over the texts listed on a slip of paper to be given free at the close of the meeting. He emphasized the importance of standing on God's Word.

The following morning I rose early, as soon as it was light enough to see. On my knees, I read from the list I have mentioned, all the texts given. But before I had gone half way down the list, I saw clearly God's Word taught, beyond a shadow of a doubt, that the overcoming, victorious life in Christ is the normal life God has planned for His children. In the two days that followed, clearer light came, with a dawning hope that this life might be possible for me. . . .

The day after reaching home, I picked up the little booklet, *The Life That Wins*, and, going to my son's bedside, I asked him to allow me to read the booklet aloud, as it was the personal testimony of Charles G. Trumbull, editor of the *Sunday School Times*, the man who had been a great blessing to me at the Conference.

As I began to read, quite a number gathered around, listening with deep interest. I read on till I came to the words: "At last I realized that Jesus Christ was actually and literally within me." I stopped amazed. The sun seemed suddenly to come from under a cloud and flood my soul with light! How blind I had been! I saw as in a flash the secret of victory. It was just Jesus Christ Himself!

But the thought of victory was for the moment lost sight of in the inexpressible joy of the new vision and realization of Christ.

For days I seemed as if in a dream. Fearing lest I be, as it were, "carried off my feet," by what had come to me, I determined to seek the advice of one, who had for many years been our beloved and honored foreign missionary secretary, the Rev. Dr. R. P. MacKay, a man known for his sanctity and common sense. (My husband was away, as I remember.)

Never can I forget a detail of that interview. Dr. MacKay listened sympathetically while I told all. I ended by saying, "Do you think I am going too far in this? I have just sent off to missionaries in China fifty copies of the booklet, *The Life That Wins*."

Dr. MacKay smiled as he replied, "No, Mrs. Goforth, for I have just sent out to ministers and others several hundred copies of the same booklet."

Then he gravely added: "Mrs. Goforth, I am amazed; amazed that you have only now come to apprehend this truth of Christ's Indwelling. You have been the wife of Jonathan Goforth for many years. His messages were aglow with this truth. It is the Holy of Holies of our Christian faith."

"Yes, Dr. MacKay," I replied humbly, "I begin to realize this and wonder at my blindness. One sentence my husband so often uses has come back to me these days: 'All the resources of the Godhead are at our disposal!'"

Dr. MacKay then said: *"It seems that this, the deepest truth, the union of the Divine and human, is not received by simple head knowledge, but must be apprehended through the Holy Spirit's revealing."* [Emphasis added]

I left Dr. MacKay strengthened in the belief that what had come to me was indeed of the Holy Spirit. But, I was determined to search the Scriptures and stand only on them. That summer I laid aside all secular reading and, with a concordance, dug into my Bible; and, oh, the wonderful treasures I found! The line of study was entirely on the union of the Divine and human.

Later I discovered that the words: "God would make known what is the riches of the glory of this mystery among the Gentiles; which is Christ in you, the hope of glory" (Col. 1:27) had changed the lives of many who later became marvelously used of God. . . .

More than twenty years have gone by since I passed through the experience of which I have just written. Many, many times in these years have I been humbled and brought low because of disobedience to the heavenly vision, but, praise God, His fountain of cleansing always has been open, and His heart of love always ready to forgive and renew. Indeed, as I look back over these past twenty years, the goodness of the Lord to me has been so great, His sustaining, protecting, guiding Presence so manifest, I seem to lose sight of my failures in the multitude of His mercies. Truly, "He hath not dealt with us after our sins; nor rewarded us according to our iniquities" (Psa. 103:10).[16]

On our journey back to China after that 1916-17 furlough, often I talked with my dear husband of the future, wondering if the Lord would ever give me the joy of knowing I had in some measure retrieved that which I knew had followed me down through the years: *"If she would only live more as she preaches."* Oh, how I longed to live so that the Chinese could see Christ in me. My impatience and quickness of speech were my besetting sins.

Many a man had I trained to be an efficient cook and really valuable servant only to lose him suddenly because of my lack of patience, giving a rebuke well deserved perhaps, but given in anger.

Many months (I forget just how long), had passed after our return to our Changte station when one evening, one of our leading evangelists came in, just when my husband was about to start for the street chapel. The evangelist showed plainly he wished to speak to my husband alone, so I left the room.

When he had gone, I returned to find my husband standing by the table with a strange look on his face. He seemed deeply moved, yet glad. I exclaimed, "Whatever is the matter?"

"Rose," he said, "you could never guess what he came for. He came as a deputation from the other evangelists and workers, yes, and servants too, to ask what is the secret of the change in you. Before you went home, none of the servants wanted to serve you, but now they all want to be your servants."

Is it any wonder tears flowed for very joy? But as if to test to the utmost, the Lord was even then preparing a furnace "seven times heated" through which in the days so soon to come, we were to pass.[17]

Dr. Goforth was called upon at aged sixty-eight to establish a new field for the Presbyterian Mission, as their former sphere of labor in Honan had been given to another mission. When the call came, Rosalind's physical outlook was far from favorable or even safe. We revert to her own description of the momentous decision she had to make at age sixty-three:

> When, after church union, the field in which we had been labor-ing became the province of the United Church and my husband was asked by our Presbyterian Board to undertake the important mission of securing a new field in China, it seemed quite out of the question that I could possibly accompany him. I was very ill; but as he stood by my couch, with the cable calling for his immediate return to China in his hand, he said, "I ought to go, but I dare not leave you as you are."
>
> For only a brief moment I closed my eyes and prayed, "Lord, show me what I should do."
>
> Then, clearly came the answer, "Go with him."
>
> Looking up, I said: "Jonathan, I'm going with you." And even as I spoke, the thought came, "I would rather die with him, when travel-ing, than die alone here."
>
> It was a step of faith, and by taking it I learned how marvelously the Lord could work for me: so much so I was even encouraged to ask for strength to deliver a brief message at our farewell meeting in Knox Church, Toronto, a few days later. This I did only by His enabling.
>
> How can I tell in one brief paragraph the story of the following nine months, traveling almost constantly, while day by day going down ever deeper into the valley of the shadow, until, at last, on a stretcher, I entered the great Rockefeller Foundation Hospital at Peking.[18]

One month in the hospital and on a strict diet saw Rose gain-ing weight once more after having lost fifty pounds in the previous eighteen months. But she was still very ill, and it was at this time that Jonathan, after having searched for months for a new field of labor, and having experienced much frustration in the process, was invited to Manchuria. He knew instinctively that this was the answer to many prayers. But we are told that "his wife lay so low in the hospital he was obliged to wait a week before the doctors gave their consent for him to leave, for, as the future proved, the lowest ebb had been reached, and the long two years' fight back to health had begun."

The costly self-denial and trust demanded of these saints in later life called forth immense courage. Manchuria was cold and distances vast. It had a winter weather pattern similar to mid-Canada, and the thermometer registered zero as the intrepid pioneers entered their new territory.

Rented premises with less guaranteed support was to be their portion for the last lap of their itinerary for God. In one station, their living conditions were so bad that they had to wear boots even in their living-room, for the earth floor became wet mud when the rains fell. Rosalind was laid low by tonsillitis followed by sciatica and lumbago, and as if that were not sufficient, this was succeeded by inflammatory rheumatism of the joints accompanied by a high fever and agonizing pain. God wonderfully answered prayer, however, for an emergency arose which necessitated their removal to a sunnier clime where they found warmer and more agreeable quarters.

Now limited in their finance, the Goforths needed a secretary to answer letters and a treasurer to keep track of unsolicited support which was coming in. Rose, unfit for more strenuous labors, fit the bill, and thus discovered a new door of usefulness open to her. There was much to do, for Jonathan had taken a further risk of faith by taking responsibility for the finance of a band of Chinese evangelists who would augment their depleted team. His faith was amply rewarded, and money was forthcoming, for the number of evangelists increased from six to sixty.

In April, 1933, Rose's husband faced the loss of valuable eyesight. Very few can understand the handicapping effect of blindness; only those who have experienced its ravages can fully realize what a mercy it has been to be able to see nature and the face and form of loved ones. But this obstacle was overcome and even turned to good, as we have related in the sketch of Jonathan Goforth.

At last, the two faithful warriors returned to Canada and when her partner of almost fifty years passed on to his reward, Rosalind began the writing of her husband's life. What a legacy she has left to us in *Goforth of China*. Her own autobiography, entitled *Climbing*, enabled us to write this sketch which, we trust, will encourage many another struggling climber to scale the heights with Christ— no matter what the cost.

Kate Lee
1872-1920

Kate Lee

S HEPHERD was drunk again, and when he got drunk he loved to fight. Throwing those fists about in the air threateningly gave him a sense of superiority. Just as he was ready to strike, he felt a light touch on his arm, and looked around to gaze into the blue eyes of a delicate, fair-haired young woman. Resentment and anger filled his breast, but they cooled as he saw an appealing look in those eyes which showed no trace of fear as she sought to separate another drunk from him. Shepherd wondered if this young woman would ever leave him alone. Sunday she had spoiled his good time by holding an open-air right on the garden plot in front of his house. It was mysterious how she would meet him on the way to work early in the morning. The "Blue Lion" (a tavern) was never a safe retreat for him any more, for Kate Lee had an uncanny way of knowing he was there, and she would make her way among the tables and chairs to where he was sprawling. It was only a few words she would speak—an invitation to a service, or just a few words about Christ's love, but it made him uncomfortable and miserable. She seemed to be everywhere. If only, he thought, she were more masculine looking or stronger built, a man might be able to change this state of affairs. But this wisp of a woman—what could he do?

Such constant efforts and prayers, however, eventually brought Shepherd to the feet of Christ, Who had shed His love abroad in Kate's heart by the Holy Ghost. She did not endeavor to foolishly labor for other souls with a human love, meant to embrace only blood ties. She received power for service and partook of a Christ-love that made it natural to mother souls who belonged to God's great family.

Speaking of Kate Lee, Harold Begbie, author and journalist, says:

> She loved the worst people in the world. The Pharisee might turn away with disgust, the judge might condemn, science might pronounce the case hopeless. She smiled and waited, waited at the prison door, waited in the pit of abomination, waited at the hard heart. And while she waited, she prayed quietly and calmly; and while she prayed, so great was the love of God in her heart, she smiled. There is no hope for the world until the love that was in Kate Lee is in us. I never looked into a human face so full of the love of God, so shining with love of humanity, as the face of this "Angel Adjutant."[1]

Kate Lee's call to love the unlovely began with a small event which, insignificant in itself, helped to decide the whole course of her life. She resided with her sister Lucy and her widowed mother in a modest little dwelling in the suburb of London. They had moved from a larger house when bereaved of their father and breadwinner.

One evening, Lucy ran to the window as the strains of music penetrated their home. Looking out on to the street below, she saw about twenty marchers making their way to an open-air service. Curious, Lucy put on her hat and followed the procession. As a result, she was brought to Christ in the indoor service that followed, conducted by the Salvation Army. Her mother, an Episcopalian, was not too pleased with her daughter's fascination with the Salvation Army and its undignified methods. The change in Lucy, however, was to influence her sister Kate, five years younger than herself, and result in her salvation and, more gradually, in her total integration into the Salvation Army.

Kate was an August baby, born in 1872. Frail in health and extremely shy by nature, there was nothing about her that could have possibly made her friends visualize the way in which God would use her in the salvaging of the outcasts of Society. Her biographer, Minnie Carpenter, gives us further insight into her character:

> General Bramwell Booth wrote of Kate Lee, "She was one of those conquering souls who seldom looked like a conqueror. She presented an extraordinary contrast. She was weak, and yet she was strong. She was poor, and yet she was one of the richest. She was intensely human with many of the most marked limitations which belong to the human, and yet she was in an extraordinary degree spiritual, yes, even divine."
>
> These contrasts were clear to all and puzzling to many. Not a few people both in and outside the ranks of The Army have asked the question, "Wherein lay the secret of Kate Lee's success?" One person, accustomed only to surface views, gave answer: "It is that she always aims to win trophies."[2]

At age seventeen, Kate enlisted full time with the Army, where she labored for thirty-one years, defying the ill health which dogged her footsteps. Someone who marveled at the quality of her converts wished to know wherein lay this frail woman's power—what was it that could capture such outcasts to Christ? Going to one of her meetings, he saw it was not her eloquence or a special gift of oratory that could possibly account for her success. However, having occasion the next morning to be on the street at an early hour, he was surprised to meet the Angel Adjutant and asked why she was out so early. He learned that the convert of the previous night would be meeting temptation at work that day, so she wished to pray and strengthen him for the fray. Upon hearing this explanation, the inquirer knew immediately that he had discovered Kate Lee's secret.

Love animated this modest, gracious, frail young woman to exhaust her own life's energies for the worst of humanity, and die penniless but happy. The same love in much greater degree made Christ leave the glories and beauties of Heaven to die ignominiously on the cross. Kate's passion for souls, souls, souls, is clearly illustrated by the following incident.

Attendance at the services was pulling hard and there was much indifference. She seemed unable to reach some of the "women of the street." One evening, Kate Lee astonished some of her friends by appearing in rags, her usually tidy hair pulled about in confusion as she marched down the street to lead an open-air and to later preach.

Some well-ordered yet fruitless Christians perhaps will disdainfully say that she loved the spectacular. But let us take a peep into her personal and private life as she struggles to obey the Spirit's promptings. Again services are pulling hard, and to her mind comes the suggestion of once again dressing in rags. To her co-worker she says, "I feel I should dress in rags and I just can't do it." This reserved, modest, unassuming young woman who naturally loves refinement and culture goes alone to her room to pray it through with her heavenly Father. Is she reminded of Christ, despised, reviled, and spat upon? Does she think of Paul, considered by his foes as the filth and offscouring of the earth? She comes out of her room with her decision made and quietly announces to her friends that she will appear in rags the next Sunday, and thus become all things to all men.

Those blue eyes, so quick to take in a situation, must have noticed how people parted on the pavement as she passed down the street dressed in dirty, torn clothing and an old pair of boots, her face soiled and her hair tumbled about. But as she stands to preach, a spectacle to the world, there is a new sense of love to man; a peculiar charm and power are in her words as she preaches the ancient but powerful Gospel of salvation from sin. Her penitent form that night is well filled, but only Kate Lee knows the struggle and cost of that evening's work. This is only one example out of many which illustrates how Kate was indeed one "who naturally cared" for the state of others.

This life of caring for souls could only be maintained by a daily partaking of Christ, as John pictures in his fifteenth chapter: "Except ye abide in me, and I in you. . . ." Prayer became the manner in which Kate sustained fresh life each day. Her fellow-workers gave evidence of this factor in her life with God, as her biographer tells us:

> Said one: "It seemed to me that she prayed without ceasing. Her life was one continual looking to God. She prayed upon rising. We prayed together after breakfast; later, she went to her room for an hour's private prayer and study; for special undertakings or emergencies she had special seasons of waiting upon God.". . .
>
> It was a great strength to her to feel that she lived in the atmosphere of prayer. When in the midst of a specially heavy battle for souls, she would write to comrades she knew had power in prayer and begged them specially to help her to fight through to victory. Very real were the powers of darkness and evil against which this frail woman set herself; sometimes they pressed her soul. She felt something of the sorrows and travail of soul of her Savior, of Whom it is written, "And being in an agony, he prayed." At times she suffered from depressions so heavy that they prostrated her. The Lieutenant (her fellow worker), continued, "At these times, all I could do was to let her feel that I was carrying on, whilst she sought her chief remedy, prayer. By and by, she would come from her room, strengthened and peaceful, ready again for the fight."[3]

We have already mentioned both her caring for souls and her prayer life as key factors in her being so used by God. There are other reasons for her outstanding usefulness. First of all, she was given over to Christ in every aspect of her life, as a Covenant found after her death revealed:

> From this first day of January do I solemnly renounce all that has had dominion over me, and every sin, and every lust, and in Thy name set myself in eternal opposition to the powers of hell.
>
> The whole frame of my nature, all the faculties of my mind, all the members of my body would I present to Thee this day, as a living sacrifice.

I consecrate myself to Thee; all my worldly possessions; and I pray Thee to give me the strength and courage to exert for Thy glory all the influence I may have over others.

Receive and wash me. Forgive all past failings, clothe me with Thy perfect righteousness, and sanctify me throughout by the power of Thy Spirit.

Help me that I may never withdraw in any point from this renewal of my consecration and covenant.

Help me to live in the Spirit of real consecration and crucifixion; and should I fail in carrying out this Covenant in all points as I ought, then, dear Lord, forgive and lead me to perfection.[4]

The Covenant was written when only twenty-five years of age, January, 1897. It was renewed twice—once when forty-six years old, two years before her Home-going, and again in the same year in which she died.

Some of the characters Kate Lee won for Christ were brought to the attention of the reading public through Harold Begbie's *Broken Earthenware,*—-the criminal, the puncher, the failure, rags and bones; these and many others thanked God for the day of consecration in the life of the Angel Adjutant. Kate's covenant with her Master had not ended in mere words, but resulted in vows fulfilled, sacrifices made, and gains counted loss for Christ's sake.

Secondly, Kate Lee could say with St. Paul, "This one thing I do." She loved the beautiful and lovely things of life, but she did not even window shop because she wished to save herself the struggle of saying "no" to things in which she could not hope to indulge in her life as a soldier of Christ. And she only allowed herself one recreation—the reading of good books— that she might have more time for souls for whom the world had no time. She also did not fulfill social engagements at the homes of the better class, not because she did not love good society, but because there were many who could fulfill such engagements, but precious few who cared about the salvation of the degraded.

This singleness of purpose also prevented Kate from marrying. Being a young woman of her character and ability, she was not without the offers of marriage, and once she almost wavered. Woman-like, her own home and some protecting strong arm to steady her in difficult times looked inviting. But she thought of the unsaved and wondered whether, if she married, she would be able to put her time at God's disposal as she could if she remained single. The young man waited for years, but Kate Lee became more and more certain that God had claimed her for His own peculiar treasure for a special purpose.

Her life, though now and again spectacular, had much more of the humble, faithful plodding in it. Sometimes, at midnight, after a preaching service, this frail woman climbed flights of stairs to "care for the dying." Moved frequently from corps to corps, she did not forget lonely souls who never got a letter from anyone. Mother-like she kept in contact. Hurried ten-minute calls were made daily to homes where she knew the pressure of life seemed unendurable, and she saw many through their trial by a quiet, kindly word. At other times, she would take a walk in the country with a young girl who, behaving like an untamed colt, needed a quiet, motherly talk about being noble and womanly. Then, as we have already seen, she often hurried out early in the morning to have a word of prayer with some new convert who must face the sneers and jeers of his work-mates.

We have previously included her covenant with God, but Kate had come to realize her need of a deeper experience with God if she were to faithfully keep that covenant. Her own words best describe her struggle to reach that place of complete rest and victory:

> Soon after I was converted, I realized a great need in my heart. I had turned my back on the old life, and my face was toward God. I had started to travel the upward way. For the first few weeks, I went with a rush, the joy of the new life within buoyed me up. I felt

as though I was walking on air. I did not feel any strain of the upward tread. But soon I began to feel the tension of the daily struggle, the weary march. There were obstacles in that way which impeded my progress. My circumstances were against me, and the influences surrounding me had a tendency to draw me from Christ.

I began to stumble and fall. The Tempter was soon at my side suggesting, "You're not converted; it's all a delusion; you would not feel as you do; you would not fail as you have done, if you were really a child of God. Give it up. It's no use trying," he argued. And, worst of all, I knew sin still existed in my heart. How often passion had broken my peace. How many times bitterness and evil had manifested themselves in my nature. Was I mistaken? Had I ever been converted? Was it all a delusion?

Just then God in His love and pity came to my heart; gave me a revelation. He not only showed me myself and my sin, but showed me my need. I needed something, and as I sat in a holiness meeting I realized that need was sanctification. For months the word sanctification was to me a heavy burden, a torture. I could not really grasp its meaning. I read and re-read the theory of sanctification, going from one authority on the subject to another, only to turn away still more puzzled. I then set myself to seek publicly and was several times found at the holiness table, pleading for the blessing that I failed to understand. Again and again I came to the altar, and as far as I understood, laid my all there. But as soon as the test came, without realizing that I did it, I took from off the altar the sins I had laid there, or the gifts that I had surrendered to God.

This is where I failed many times, and during my officership, I have found scores of other souls who have failed on this very point. They come sincerely to the altar, definitely laying their gift there, a living sacrifice; but when the knife is felt, the realization of the dying comes upon them as they feel the hurt and understand fully what it means, they shrink and draw back. Abraham's experience, related in Genesis 15 has been a great help to me. He had to wait for the fire. He prayed all day, even until eventide, and then the birds of prey came down; but he stood by the sacrifice and drove them off. Then the fire came and consumed the sacrifice.

That was just the point to which I had to get. I had laid my all on the altar, but then I had to wait for the fire. Meanwhile, the birds of doubt, fear, and discouragement came flying around. I had to get up again and again to drive them off, and hold on to God.

Fresh light came; a new path opened up. The laying of self on the altar meant following God fully and showing my colors everywhere. Could I do it? It was hard to die to self, and say, "Yes, Lord." But as I said it, I felt I was accepted, and afterwards, when I carried out that vow, joy flooded my soul and I realized that the Spirit of the Lord was upon me. The desire to sin was removed, and my heart yearned to be kept pure and clean.

I have found the need of great watchfulness and have needed much prayer to keep my soul in touch with God and on fire for precious souls. Although I realized, after I was sanctified . . . that I was cleansed from the desire to sin, yet in his subtlety the devil has come again and again and striven to bring me down.

Sometimes he has come as an angel of light, so that I have been led to the very verge of sin, tempted to indulge in what seemed at the moment harmless, perhaps because others, who professed as much as I did, indulged in it too. Tempted to shrink from the sacrifice that a separated life must mean; tempted to give way to the flesh, one's natural desires and inclinations, I have even allowed the devil to take me to the edge of a great spiritual precipice, but God in His mercy has flashed His wonderful light upon my path in time to show me where I was, and what would be the outcome if I yielded to the temptation. Oh, how it caused me to pray and seek strength which enabled me to overcome!

Prayer has been my source of help, when burdens have pressed so heavily upon me that they threatened to crush my spirit; when disappointments, misrepresentations almost overwhelmed me, prayer has brought strength and comfort, a courage that could face a world of bitterness and scorn. I have proved that prayer will enable me to retain the substance of holiness. Prayer enables me to retain a passion for souls; keeps it burning in hours of disappointment and failure, indifference and hardness, when men and devils rise in power against me.

One must tread the path of holiness carefully, with a watchful eye and ear always open to His voice, and a spirit ever ready to obey. But it is a wonderful way, a way of purity, where the soul can see God, even in the struggles of life. A way of joy; the deepest of joys. The realization of His smile enables me to live independent of all the joys of the world and to rejoice in the hour of sorrow. A way of power; when the channel is clear He works through it and accomplishes His will.[5]

Lest we think Kate Lee a super-woman, not touched with the same trials and temptations as we are, let us read how she coped with bitterness and an unforgiving spirit:

> This life was not spasmodic. She did not pass in and out of the Holy Place, or step on and off the Highway of Holiness. She dwelt there. That does not imply that never during those years was she overcome by Satan. Once, into a deep sorrow was poured the bitterness of gall through the wickedness of another. The enemy came in like a flood, threatening to overwhelm and root up many precious things, but the Spirit of the Lord was there to lift up a standard against him.
>
> "If ye forgive not men their trespasses, neither will your Father forgive your trespasses," was the word that came to her heart. She closed her lips, hushed her sobs, and crept to the feet of her Lord, where are ever the prints of cruel nails to remind His children of His sufferings and His forgiveness.
>
> "I was wrong," she said, "very wrong. I must forgive, I do forgive." And to the close of her life she lavished love upon one who had sore wounded her. "If any man sin, we have an Advocate. . . ." She laid her case in His hands, and left it there.[6]

Her ill health finally became the autocratic dictator demanding that this untiring but frail worker retire from her active ministry. Her last days on earth, however, were filled with endeavoring to pass on to others her commission to love earth's unlovely. She was only in her prime, but she had finished her work. Lucy, her sister, leaned over her as she lay dying. "Oh, the people, the people! I haven't the heart to send them away," moaned Kate. Lucy endeavored to soothe her by telling her that her whole life had been given for them, but she only moaned, "I haven't the heart to send them away." Even in pain, her thoughts were for the Christless multitudes.

The "Angel Adjutant" had fought a good fight and finished her course on March 8, 1920. The streets were lined with thousands the day they carried her to her last resting place. In life, Kate Lee had indeed "won her trophies," but now she has laid her trophies at the feet of the One Who truly understands the worth of an immortal soul.

W. Graham Scroggie
1877-1954?

Graham Scroggie

D R. Grattan Guinness was expecting the speaker who was to take the Bible readings at the Keswick Convention. But he was bewildered as he surveyed the strange-looking young man with the tousled hair, who had lost his hat while en route to this appointment and had borrowed one much too small. Could this be the chosen speaker for this large world-wide convention? Could this be the man to give the Bible readings to the thousands gathered there? But Graham Scroggie, as we shall see, had been through a process where appearances meant little to him, and he did not disappoint the expectations of many souls hungering for living bread as they listened to his illuminated messages. Twelve times was he to return to Keswick as the Bible teacher.

"When Heaven is about to confer a great office on a man it always first exercises his mind and soul with suffering, and his body to hunger, and exposes him to extreme poverty, and baffles all his undertakings. By these means it stimulates his mind, hardens his nature, and enables him to do acts otherwise not possible to him." So wrote Mencius, the Chinese sage, two thousand years ago. And as we peruse the biographies of great musicians, painters, and authors, who have left a heritage of beauty and usefulness behind them, we recognize the truth of the above. But if this be so in the non-Christian realm, how much more does this hold true of those who seek to turn men from darkness to light and from the power of Satan unto God.

Dr. W. Graham Scroggie illustrated the above truth, for his arduous climb to usefulness in the ministry was up toilsome ascents in lonely places before he could be used to minister bread to the many hungry who gathered yearly at the Keswick Convention for spiritual help.

Both of his parents were of Scottish nationality, although Graham was born in England. He was surrounded from infancy by a spiritual atmosphere, and the "mantle of the prophetic office was draped around his shoulders" when only nine years old.

The story of his parents' romance is fascinating. His father, a young evangelist, had no settled income on which to start married life, and, in addition, was experiencing serious health problems. This made his fiancée's parents seriously question his suitability as a future son-in-law. It troubled them most that he had no definite means of finance. Alice Cook, in a short sketch of Jeannie Scroggie's life, tells of this love-story and its consequences:

"It was thought," wrote Mrs. Scroggie in later years, "that my father had done a foolish thing in allowing his daughter to think of marrying one who had no settled home or income, but all that had no effect on my mind though I felt sorry for my parents."

No settled home! No settled income! No responsible organization or society! Here was one of the real adventurous love stories of the world. But these lovers could afford to be so. They ran a risk. They had their secret. They believed their joyous planning was in accordance with the divine purpose. After her marriage, the bride wrote in retrospect, "It was neither the love of our hearts, nor the reason of our dear parents, that was to prevail, but the will of God."

. . . Mrs. Scroggie had definite convictions regarding the guided life. "Do we really believe," she asked "that our lives in detail are appointed of God, and that not to follow His plan for us is to court failure? . . . Our way was made clear, and although the place to which we went was not one which we would have chosen had the choice been left to us, it was unmistakably the place of His appointing, and that sufficed."

While ministering for the Lord in Annan, Scotland, Graham's parents underwent most severe trials, losing four of their children from a violent form of scarlet fever. And as though this were not

enough, the father succumbed to the disease and lay partially para-
lyzed from the fever for twelve months. The skill and love of a
doctor helped to bring him back when his life had been more than
once despaired of. What a help-mate James Scroggie had found in
Jeannie, who, with her Scotch granite character, fulfilled her duty
cheerfully, and was not deterred by trouble or tragedy!

More than once, they realized the loss of all things for Christ's
sake, and their devotion to Him enabled them, under His direction, to shape young Graham's life into an instrument to be used
by the Master. Training under such godly parents who risked all in
order to do God's will left an indelible impression upon the young
boy. What infinite pains does God take in sharpening His tools so
that they may be skillfully used!

In addition to this background of parental example, William
Graham had the privilege to be trained under Spurgeon and proved
to be an unusually gifted scholar. Everything appeared to his advantage, and there were those that prophesied that he would go far
in his calling. But God does not think as man does. His thoughts
are infinitely higher than man's thoughts, so instead of success, the
young man was given severe testings and discipline.

His youthful dreams of fame were shattered when his first appointment proved seemingly disastrous. He was dismissed from
his church; he was unwanted! And that would not have been so
hard to bear had he been single, but he was now married with a
home and wife to maintain. For two years he was unemployed
with no tangible means of income. In later life, he had this to say
about this trying period:

> I have been dismissed twice. People said, "How sad!" Nothing of
> the kind! My two dismissals were the sources of all the blessing which
> has run through my life. After my second dismissal, I had a rich op-
> portunity to study the Word of God; during these two years the foun-
> dations were laid for all the Bible work I have done since.
>
> Only once in those two years did a meal time arrive when there
> was nothing in the house to eat, but within half-an-hour of the usual

time a basket was handed in. I took off the cover and on a dish was a chicken covered with sauce and sausages all around, and some other things—sweets of one kind or another.

A friend writing of this period said, "That time passed and Graham Scroggie was called to another church. But the cup was not yet full, the testing not done. Wise craftsmen take infinite pains with their best work and spare neither refining pot nor chisel to perfect their art. And could God do less than remake, mold, and shape the life that was to be a masterpiece to the praise of His glory?"

While attending a Convention for the deepening of the Christian life, Graham Scroggie passed through a deep soul crisis; for he realized that although he had learned how to preach, he had not learned the secret of victorious living. He was spiritually bankrupt, and for two years he knew deep travail of soul as he sought the Lord. He described this period, or we should have been the poorer for lack of knowledge of this advance in his Christian life.

> Can I ever forget the time long ago, when my whole life and ministry was suddenly challenged; when it was revealed to me that I was little more than a middle man between my books and my people; when it dawned on me I was more anxious to be a preacher than to be God's messenger; that my master-passion was not to accomplish the will of God at any cost, and that my ruling motive was not the love of Christ?
>
> In that hour, the edifice I had been building lay in ruins about me, and for a while all was dark despair. But "into the wood my Master came," and finding me there He, in His mercy, brought me out, out into newness of life, out into fullness of service. . . . I gratefully bear testimony to His coming then in that way. It has been the determining factor of my life. It was during these years I discovered the vital distinction between the Saviorship and the Mastership of Jesus Christ. Yielding to the Mastership of Christ has been my outstanding spiritual experience. If we accept Him as Master we may look for trouble, because His plan for our life may cut across every plan we have made for ourselves! God has not promised His people a smooth voyage—only a safe landing.

Heaven is not always angry when He strikes,
But He most chastises those whom most He likes.

That air of confidence, that touch of arrogance was melted as dross in God's refining fires and the old Graham Scroggie was no more. He was now yielded and still in Another's hands to be made into the pattern of God's design and purpose. "All his most precious things, his oratory, his literary gifts, his unusually powerful intellect, were all laid at his Master's feet, to be used by Him."

Having learned through experience that Christ was Master, he was enabled to write and preach on the theme of abundant life in Christ. His excellent Bible readings from the Old Testament book of Joshua, delivered at the Keswick Convention and later published in book form, show the parallels between the entrance into this life more abundant and the journey of the children of Israel from Egypt into Canaan. In my estimation, this commentary on Joshua is one of the most spiritual and edifying that I have read. We have taken some extracts from this book to show the depth of Dr. Scroggies' revelation and understanding:

The way of the fully yielded life is not one of escapism, but is one of conflict issuing in victory; the life of rest is a life of unceasing action and boundless energy.

The life to which we are called is not a glorified picnic, but a warfare.

Heights are dangerous places. Only a steady hand can carry a full cup. In Jesus' experience, after the Dove came the Devil; after the divine attestation came the diabolical attack; and can we suppose that it can be otherwise with ourselves?

Fresh light is given only to the obedient; and direction in the way is given only to those who have faithfully followed past guidance.

To slacken our interest and energy in spiritual advancements is to grieve the Holy Spirit, to rob ourselves of blessing, to hinder other people, and to encourage the enemy. No Christian will win a race who stops to take a breather; nor will he win a fight, who asks for compassionate leave.

Capacity is not something rigid, like an iron box, but something supple and elastic; it is a faculty that becomes larger with use. The more anyone has of Christ, the more he is capable of having. If we grasp all of Him that is within our reach today, there will be more of Him for us to grasp tomorrow.

When all the resources of the Almighty are at our disposal, it is not only foolishness, but wickedness to give up and admit defeat.

Compromise is the endeavor to make the best of incompatibles, and this is fatal alike in the regenerate person, and in the Christian Church. The devil's attack upon Jesus in the wilderness was an attempt to get Him to compromise His faith, in the matter of the bread; His reason, in the matter of falling from the pinnacle of the temple; and His conscience, in the matter of whom He should worship; and Jesus hurled back the temptation at every point.

These are still the cardinal points of compromise. Every Christian who is compromising is doing so, either by withdrawing from simple faith in God, or by abandoning his common sense for popularity, or by violating his conscience for temporary gain, and such compromise is always fatal.

The church that sets out to spiritualize the world will soon find that the world will secularize the church. When wheat and tares compromise, it is the wheat that suffers. Light and darkness, right and wrong, good and evil, truth and error are incompatibles, and when they compromise it is the light, the right, the good, and the truth that are damaged.

In our time, in place of the "lot" are the Holy Spirit, the Word of God, the Throne of Grace, and the open or closed door, that is, circumstances. By these means we may discover what God's will for us is, and if we are subject to them, these means will never fail us. . . . If a Christian does not believe in a divine unerring providence, Who guides in all the minor, as in all the major affairs of life, he cannot as he should, possess his inheritance in Christ.

It is the discrepancy between our profession and our experience that needs looking to; and we must deal with it, not in the twilight of past attainment but in the noontide of divine possibility.

Every superstructure must have a foundation, but every foundation should have a superstructure; and revelation and experience stand much in this relation to one another. Experience which does not rest on revealed truth is bound to mislead, and may prove fatal; and a knowledge of revealed truth which does not find embodiment in joyful experience, leaves men cold, and often makes them cruel.

We should ever remember that doctrine is not the measure of experience, but only its mold; and we must remember also, that experience is not the standard of truth but only its apprehension and appropriation.[1]

In a sermon about the temptation of Christ in the wilderness which appeared in *The Life of Faith* in 1923, Dr. Scroggie's words are weighty because the prophet had become, through experience, his own message. We give a few extracts, praying they may bless the reader:

He who most closely follows God will be most closely followed by the devil. Never can we engage in any act of true surrender without exposing ourselves to the onslaught of the great foe. You have but to pursue the path of loyal obedience to the known will of God and you shall certainly have Diabolus in hot pursuit of you. . . . It is only to be expected that anointing shall be followed by assault, and after the Dove shall come the devil. . . . The devil always most opposes those whom God most approves.

It is those who are obedient, endowed, and well-pleasing to God who are the especial objects of the enemy's stratagems. To be left unmolested by Satan is no evidence of spiritual vigor. Seasons of fiercest temptation frequently follow seasons of greatest blessing. Worship is often the path to war. But to fully apprehend the significance of this struggle we must see it not only as coming after, but also before momentous events. . . .

We should ever remember that it is in private that we are prepared for our defeats or victories in public. While bearing in mind the peculiar perils of solitude we cannot overestimate its educative value. Foundations are always out of sight, and it is ever in seclusion from the crowd that foundations of character or service, good or evil, are laid.

Dr. Helen Roseveare had been a Christian for only a short time when she was privileged to sit under the ministry of Dr.

Scroggie. He wrote in her new Bible the verse Philippians 3:10: "That I may know Him"—and he added "You have come there; and I pray that you will go on to know 'the power of His resurrection.'" He paused and then looking her straight in the face, he added, "And one day you may be privileged to know something of 'the fellowship of his sufferings.'"

This statement proved prophetic, for twenty years later, Dr. Roseveare was the first white to be captured during the rebellion of 1964 in the Congo. She was beaten with a rubber truncheon and cruelly kicked, losing some of her teeth. Alone, she was at the mercy of her cruel attackers. She cried out to God that she could bear no more, when suddenly she was reminded that twenty years previous, she had told Him she would accept the privilege of fellowship with His suffering. Her fears were stilled, and she knew God was there, taking her suffering with her.

> Great truths are greatly won. Not found by chance,
>   Nor wafted on the breath of summer dream,
> But grasped in the great struggle of the soul,
>   Hard buffetings with adverse wind and stream.
>
> Not in the general mart, 'mid corn and wine,
>   Not in the merchandise of gold and gems,
> Not in the world's gay halls of midnight mirth,
>   Not 'mid the blaze of regal diadems;
>
> But in the day of conflict, fear, and grief,
>   When the strong hand of God, put forth in might,
> Plows up the subsoil of the stagnant heart,
>   And brings the imprisoned truth-seed to the light.
>
> Wrung from the troubled spirit in hard hours
>   Of weakness, solitude, perchance of pain,
> Truth springs, like harvest, from the well-plowed field,
>   And the soul feels it has not wept in vain.
>   —*Horatius Bonar.*

We have no record before us of the later trials which attended Dr. Scroggie's pathway. We do not doubt but that if he were the writer of this sketch he would share with us those experiences which would confirm the words of Jesus that "all that will live godly in Christ Jesus shall suffer persecution."

Notes to Sources

1. George Herbert
1. John J. Daniell, *The Life of George Herbert of Bemerton*, (London: SPCK, 1902) p. 193
2. Ibid., p. 193
3. Rev. Robert Aris Willmott (Ed.) *The Works of George Herbert in Prose and Verse*, (London: George Routledge and Co., 1857) p. XX

2. Miguel Molinos
1. *Golden Thoughts*, p. 37
2. Ibid., p. 10
3. Ibid., pp. 11,12
4. Ibid., pp. 90-91

3. Joseph Alleine
1. Robert Steele, *Burning and Shining Lights*, p. 41
2. Ibid., p. 26
3. Richard Baxter (Ed.) *The Life and Death of that Excellent Minister of Christ Mr. Joseph Alleine*, (London: Nevil Simons, 1672) pp.18-20
4. Steele, p. 27
5. Baxter, p. 115
6. Ibid., pp. 33-39
7. Ibid., p. 102
8. Ibid., p. 114
9. Ibid., p. 120
10. Ibid., Letters Section, pp. 1-7
11. Ibid., p. 30
12. Steele, p. 36
13. Baxter, pp. 62-63

14. Ibid., p. 63 & p. 68
15. Ibid., pp. 102-103
16. Steele, p. 39
17. Ibid., p. 39
18. Baxter, p. 65
19. Steele, p. 40
20. Baxter, p. 90
21. Ibid., p 94
22. Ibid., pp. 95-96
23. Ibid., p. 98
24. Ibid., p. 99
25. This and subsequent letter extracts are from the Letters Section of Baxter's *The Life and Death, etc.*
26. Ibid., p. 73
27. Ibid., pp 142-144

4. John Fletcher
1. Joseph Benson, The Life of John Fletcher, (Salem, Ohio: Allegheny Publications, 1984) pp. 17-18
2. Ibid., pp. 21-22
3. Ibid., p. 28
4. Ibid., pp. 23-25
5. Ibid., p. 27
6. Ibid., p. 32
7. Jabez Marrat, John Fletcher—Saint and Scholar, (London: Charles H. Kelly, 1902) pp. 18-20
8. Benson, p. 55
9. Ibid., pp. 58-61
10. Ibid., p. 66
11. Ibid., p. 67
12. Ibid., p. 68
13. Ibid., p. 59
14. Ibid., p. 75
15. Ibid., pp. 138-9

16. Ibid., p. 144
17. Ibid., p. 144
18. Ibid., p. 145
19. Ibid., p. 145
20. Ibid., pp. 145-7
21. Bishop Cannon, Theology of John Wesley, p. 146
22. Benson, p. 149
23. Ibid., p. 149
24. Ibid., pp. 175-7
25. Ibid., p. 284
26. Ibid., pp. 286-7
27. Ibid., pp. 296-7
28. Henry Moore, The Life of Mrs. Mary Fletcher, (London: John Mason, 1844) pp. 169-176

5. Mary Fletcher

1. Henry Moore, *The Life of Mrs. Mary Fletcher,* (London: John Mason, 1844) p. 324
2. *The Burning Bush,* April 16, 1953
3. Moore, p. 34
4. Ibid., p. 141
5. Ibid., pp. 324-5
6. Ibid., pp. 160-1
7. Ibid., p. 165
8. Ibid., pp. 169-171
9. Ibid., pp. 165-6
10. Ibid., p. 235
11. Ibid., pp. 185-9
12. Ibid., pp. 186-7
13. Ibid., p. 244
14. Ibid., p. 334
15. Ibid., p. 338
16. Ibid., p. 341
17. Ibid., p. 349

18. Ibid., p. 365
19. Ibid., p. 143
20. Ibid., p. 293
21. Ibid., p. 357
22. Ibid., p. 350
23. Ibid., pp. 335-6
24. Ibid., p. 281
25. Ibid., p. 327
26. Ibid., p. 275
27. Ibid., p. 262
28. Ibid., p. 259
29. *The Burning Bush* ,1951

6. Frederick Oberlin
1. *Memoirs of John Frederic Oberlin,* compiled from authentic sources, (London: Holdsworth and Ball, 1830) pp. 50-52
2. Ibid., p. 217
3. Ibid., pp. 236-237
4. Ibid., p. 103
5. Ibid., p. 122
6. Ibid., p. 100
7. Ibid., pp. 151-155
8. Ibid., p. 274
9. R. W. Chambers on Oberlin
10. *Memoirs,* pp. 181-2
11. Ibid., pp. 194-5
12. Ibid., pp. 291-302

7. Samuel Pollard
1. Rev. W. A. Grist, *Samuel Pollard, Pioneer Missionary in China,* (London: United Methodist Publishing House) p. 18
2. Ibid., p. 19
3. Ibid., p. 32
4. Ibid., p. 33

5. Ibid., p. 37-8
6. Ibid., p. 43
7. Ibid., p. 60
8. Ibid., p. 88
9. Ibid., p.102
10. Ibid., p. 109
11. Ibid., p. 109
12. Ibid., p. 181

8. George Matheson
1. George Matheson, *Searchings in the Silence,* (London: Hodder and Stoughton) p. 166
2. Ibid., 93-95
3. D. Macmillan, *The Life of George Matheson,* (London: Hodder and Stoughton, 1910) pp. 120-121
4. Ibid., pp. 121-2
5. Ibid., pp. 123-4
6. Ibid., pp. 117-118
7. *Searchings in the Silence,* p. 42
8. *The Life of George Matheson,* pp. 242-4
9. Ibid., p. 282
10. Ibid., pp. 328-9
11. *Searchings in the Silence,* p. 157
12. Ibid., pp. 89-90
13. Ibid., p. 114
14. *The Life of George Matheson,* p. 50

9. Jonathan Goforth
1. Rosalind Goforth, *Goforth of China,* (Grand Rapids: Zondervan Publishing House, 1939) pp. 24-5
2. Ibid., pp. 27-8
3. Ibid., p. 33
4. Ibid., pp. 87-8
5. Ibid., p. 83

6. Ibid., pp. 194-7
7. Ibid., p. 270 & p. 355
8. Ibid., pp. 270-1
9. Ibid., p. 304
10. Ibid., p. 314
11. Ibid., pp. 232-4
12. Ibid., pp. 310-11
13. Ibid., pp. 318-19

10. Rosalind Goforth
1. Rosalind Goforth, *Climbing*, (Toronto: Evangelical Publishers, 1940) pp. 10-11
2. Ibid., pp. 14-16
3. Ibid., p. 19
4. Rosalind Goforth, *Goforth of China*, (Grand Rapids: Zondervan Publishing House, 1939) pp. 47-49
5. *Climbing*, pp. 21-3
6. *Goforth of China*, pp. 75-6
7. *Climbing*, pp. 41-2
8. *Goforth of China*, pp. 76-7
9. Ibid., pp. 89-90
10. Ibid., pp. 158-9
11. *Climbing*, pp 75-8
12. Ibid., p. 169
13. Ibid., pp. 50-52
14. Ibid., pp. 84-6
15. Ibid., pp. 86-9
16. Ibid., pp. 192-199
17. Ibid., pp. 202-3
18. Ibid., pp. 204-5

11. Kate Lee
1. Minnie Lindsay Carpenter, *Kate Lee: 'The Angel Adjutant'*, (London, Salvationist Publishing, 1950) p. 82
2. Ibid., pp. 90-91

3. Ibid., pp. 96-7
4. Ibid., pp. 92-3
5. Ibid., pp. 93-6
6. Ibid., p. 96

12. W. Graham Scroggie

1. This and the preceding quotations are from W. Graham Scroggie, *The Land and Life of Rest*, (London: Pickering and Inglis, 1957)

OTHER VOLUMES AVAILABLE

They Knew Their God
by E. F. & L. Harvey and E. Hey

VOLUME ONE
Characters included:

- Nicholas of Basle
- John Tauler
- Christmas Evans
- William Bramwell
- Mother Cobb
- Felix Neff
- Robert Cleaver Chapman
- Holy Ann
- Isaac Marsden
- Alfred Cookman
- Elizabeth Baxter
- Lilias Trotter
- John Hyde
- Samuel Logan Brengle
- Eva Von Winkler
- Samuel Morris
- Iva Vennard
- Johanna Veenstra

VOLUME TWO
Characters included:

- Gerhard Tersteegen
- John Woolman
- Elijah Hedding
- Robert Aitken
- Mrs. Phoebe Palmer
- Robert Murray McCheyne
- William Burns
- Frances R. Havergal
- Pastor Hsi
- G. D. Watson
- Jessie Penn-Lewis
- The Three Garratt Sisters
- Paget Wilkes
- Basil Malof
- Thomas R. Kelly
- John and Betty Stam
- G. H. Lang

They Knew Their God
by E. F. & L. Harvey

VOLUME THREE
Characters included:

- Marquis De Renty
- Stephen Grellet
- Samuel Pearce
- John Smith
- Ann Cutler
- John Vassar
- George Railton
- John Govan
- Oswald Chambers
- Gertrude Chambers
- Evan Hopkins
- Mary Mozley
- Francis Asbury

VOLUME FOUR
Characters included:

- Philip and Matthew Henry
- Freeborn Garrettson
- Catherine Garrettson
- John Gossner
- John Hunt
- Elizabeth Prentiss
- Lord Radstock
- Dr. Frederick Baedeker
- Frank Crossley
- Emily Crossley
- Mathilde Wrede
- Henrietta Soltau
- James Caughey

VOLUME SIX
Characters included:

- John Chrysostom
- John Brown
- Charles Simeon
- Henry Martyn
- Helen Ewan
- Edward Payson
- James Turner
- Thomas Waring
- Anthony Norris Groves
- Mary Bethia Groves
- William Wilberforce
- John Pierpont
- Johann Christoph Blumhardt
- E. M. Bounds

Kneeling We Triumph
Volumes One & Two
Compiled by E. F. & L. Harvey
A few titles are: "Authority to Take," "Prayers that Outlive an Age," "For the Asking," "Waiting, a Proof of our Faith," "Hush My Heart to Listen," "When Prayer is a Cry." *127 pages each*

How They Prayed Series
Volume One—Household Prayers
by E. F. & L. Harvey
This book is a plea for a return of prayer and worship in the home, citing many examples of how praying family members have prevailed with God for their loved ones. Read of parents who prayed for their children, children who prayed for their parents, wives and husbands who prayed for their partners. 19 short, easy-to-read chapters. *119 pages*

Volume Two—Ministers' Prayers
by E. F. & L. Harvey
The first three chapters of this book contain testimonies from various Christians on the benefits of early morning rising for prayer and Bible study. The remaining chapters reveal the emphasis given to prayer in the lives of ministers and preachers from differing denominational backgrounds and nationalities. *104 pages*

Volume Three—Missionaries and Revival
by E. F. & L. Harvey
Read the touching story of Lily Roberts, a missionary in the Congo, who prayed, "Lord, my life for revival," and how God took her at her word. Discover how largely prayer figured in the revival of 1857 and others. Gain an insight into the prayer-lives of various missionaries. *127 pages*

Royal Exchange
Compiled by E. F. & L. Harvey
Thirty-one daily readings which stimulate the reader to exchange his/her weakness for divine strength—an exchange which seems to be the missing dimension of prayer in this busy age. *64 pages*

Asking Father
by E. F. & L. Harvey & Trudy Harvey Tait
A series of short, factual stories which inspire children to approach their Heavenly Father with confidence, knowing that He will honor their prayers. Parents enjoy reading this book as much as their children. It is also an excellent source of material for Sunday Schools. *120 pages*

The Velvet Curtain Series
by, Trudy Harvey Tait.

In writing The Velvet Curtain and its sequel Behind the Velvet Curtain, I fulfilled my long-cherished desire to write something that would help Christians live out their faith in a materialistic and amoral society. The Iron Curtain may have indeed fallen, yet its Western counterpart still makes itself felt in every land where freedom professes to hold sway.

The Velvet Curtain 336 pages

Leaving the Iron Curtain behind forever, Esther has no idea that she has merely exhcanged one Curtain for another...

Behind The Velvet Curtain 304 pages

Esther and Gabby, the two Romanian girls who, escape the Iron Curtain find themselves enmeshed in its Western counterpart. Esther takes drastic measures to stay clear of the Velvet Curtain while Gabby denies its very existence and calls it, instead, The American Dream.

Escaping The Velvet Curtain 272 pages

Esther, her sister Gabby, and their friends explore various ways in which each of them can escape the Velvet Curtain. Writing this book has made me retrace my own spiritual pilgrimage. I realize afresh that God puts us in a seemingly impossible position and then delights to deliver us when He sees that our trust is in Him alone.

If, like myself, you often wish that life was less complex, then you will empathize with Gabby, Aaron, and their friends, as they make momentous choices, often not knowing where God is leading them. And when the story takes unpredictable twists and turns, it is because God's grace is producing miracles in the lives of flawed and erring individuals, often, however, upsetting the smooth flow of their earth-bound existence.

Order online at: http:// www.harveycp.com

www.ingramcontent.com/pod-product-compliance
Lightning Source LLC
LaVergne TN
LVHW011418080426
835512LV00005B/127